AF600517

THE CATHOLIC UNIVERSITY OF AMERICA
CANON LAW STUDIES

No. 303

THE PARTICULAR PENAL PRECEPT

A DISSERTATION

Submitted to the Faculty of the School of Canon Law of the Catholic University of America in Partial Fulfillment of the Requirements for the Degree of
DOCTOR OF CANON LAW

by the

REV. HUGH GABRIEL QUINN, A. B., J. C. L.
Priest of the Diocese of El Paso

THE CATHOLIC UNIVERSITY OF AMERICA PRESS
WASHINGTON, D. C.
1953

Nihil obstat:

Ludovicus Motry, S.T.D., J.C.D.,
Censor Deputatis
Washingtonii, D. C., die 12 iunii 1951

Imprimatur:

S. M. Metzger, S.T.D., J.C.D.,
Episcopus Elpasensis
Elpasensi, 19 Octobris 1951

Printed by
REVISTA CATOLICA
El Paso, Texas

TABLE OF CONTENTS

Chapter III

Chapter IV

Chapter V

Chapter VI

Chapter VII

DEDICATED

IN THE NAME OF THE MOST HOLY TRINITY

AND OF

THE BLESSED MOTHER OF GOD

FOREWORD

The canonical penal precept is an interesting and fitting prescript of law not only for the Church in general but also in a special way for the Church in this country. Pertaining to criminal procedure, it provides ecclesiastical authority with a suitable and effective means for the prompt and facile maintenance of discipline through the timely prevention of waywardness and reprehensible conduct on the part of all subjects and especially of clerics. Vigilant and paternal superiors are able to correct situations which left unchecked would tend not only to the spiritual ruin of the individual but also to the disturbance of the harmony and sanctity of the general body of the faithful wrought by unrestrained and scandalous conduct. The canonical penal precept is admirably suited to the prevention and correction of abuse before it becomes well known and before scandal wreaks its havoc.

The supreme law of the salvation of souls is well protected and fortified through the canonical penal precept, since it primarily seeks to remove the occasions of wrongdoing effect the early repentance and return to a better life, before one can be snared in serious crime, and prevent the spread of knowledge of evil doing.

In a special way, the canonical penal precept is peculiarly suited to this country and to places where the paucity of priests and canonists hinders the complete and conventional adherence to the formal criminal procedures. The formal criminal procedure tends to be more public than the informal. In lands such as ours, the publication of a trial and sentence may occasion scandal and the *admiratio populi*. Recourse to the extrajudicial process by precept would serve to obviate much of this objection. At the same time, strict adherence to the few essential demands of the process would safeguard the individual against arbitrary and peremptory punishment without chance to plead, offer excuse, or to contest evidence which may not have beeen revealed to him.

The canonical penal precept, however, presents many problems. It is not clearly or fully delineated in the Code of Canon Law. It would be true to say that as a legal institute it is still in the early stages of formation. There is no indication in the law itself of the connections of the various canons which treat of penal precept. It is noteworthy that the substantive aspects of the law on precepts are contained in Book IV of the Code, while the adjective norms are in Book V. The opinions of authors are widely varied and in this matter, since the law is not sufficiently explicit, the jurisprudence of canonists constitutes great weight.

It has been necessary to adopt a definite opinion which seemed most in accord with parallel passages in the Code, and to use this as a standard by which to measure other interpretations. The assumption is that canon 2310, which treats of precept as a penal remedy, canon 1933, § 4 which lists the penalties which can be inflicted by precept and canon 2225, the form of precept in inflicting a penalty are logically and necessarily connected. Related questions, such as whether precepts are *a iure* or *ab homine,* and the reservation of penalties inflicted by precept are treated cursorily and only to render the study substantially complete.

The writer is greatly indebted and respectfully grateful to His Excellency, The Most Reverend Sidney M. Metzger, Bishop of El Paso, for the opportunity and encouragement in pursuing advanced studies at the Catholic University; to the members of the Faculty of the School of Canon Law for their counsel, guidance and interest; to those who generously assisted in typing and preparing the manuscript; and to all fellow students and classmates, who, by advice and assistance, have made the completion of this work possible.

PART ONE

HISTORICAL SYNOPSIS

CHAPTER ONE

THE PRE-CODE LEGISLATION

INTRODUCTION

The term, the canonical penal precept, bears several connotations. In its broadest sense it includes any use of precept as it is variously found in Book V of the Code of Canon Law. More restrictively it denotes the usage of precept as a preventive penal remedy, [1] or as an institute of procedure, that is, in the infliction of a penalty. [2]

The right to issue a precept in any of these connections flows from the right of jurisdiction possessed by legitimately constituted authority. It is a right derived from fundamental legislative authority, whose commands are duly enacted through the various institutes namely laws, statutes and precepts.

The principles pertaining to precept in common are contained in canon 24 and, apart from the exception governing the form of precept given in canon 2225, apply to the penal precept. Thus, by reason of *extension,* precepts are personal. By reason of *duration,* they are temporary or perpetual. By *mode,* precepts are paternal [3] or coercive. Coercive precepts are either preventive [4] or repressive. [5]

Thus a penal precept is either an attempt to effect the correction of or to break the contumacy of a delinquent and by threat of penalty to deter him from a crime which he might otherwise commit, or it is the actual penalizing, *per*

---

1 *Codex Iuris Canonici Pii X Pontificis Maximi iussu digestus Benedicti Papae XV auctoritate promulgatus* (Romae: Typis Polyglottis Vaticanis, 1917, Reimpressio, 1933), Canon 2310.

2 Canon 1933, § 4.

3 Canons 2307 - 2309.

4 Canon 2310.

5 Canon 1933, § 4.

modum praecepti, of a delinquent for the transgression of a precept.

To signify these concepts, two Instructions of the Holy See used similar terms. Thus the Instruction of the Sacred Congregation of Bishops and Regulars, issued on June 11, 1880, spoke of *"remedia... alia praeveniunt, alia reprimunt et medelam afferunt".* [6] The purpose of praeventive remedies is *"ut impediant quominus malum adveniat, ut scandali stimuli, occasiones voluntariae, causaeque ad delinquendum proximae removeantur".* On the other hand, repressive remedies *"finem habent revocandi delinquentes ut sapiant reparentque admissi criminis consequentias".*

An Instruction of the Sacred Congregation for the Propagation of the Faith, issued three years later, spoke of *remedia praeventiva et repressiva,* and defined them in almost the same way as the prior Instruction. For the purpose or end of the repressive remedies, the Sacred Congregation stated that they were constituted *"ut delinquentes ad bonam frugem revocentur, ac culparum consectaria e medio tollantur".* [7]

As now contained in the Code of Canon Law, a precept as a preventive is aptly defined by Coronata as "a command given by a legitimate ecclesiastical superior, by which there is accurately indicated what the subject ought to do or what he must avoid, together with a threat of penalty for transgression." [8] The procedure of inflicting a penalty by means of a precept is briefly explained by the same author. "To inflict a penalty by way of a precept is the same as inflicting a penalty not contained in any law or general precept, but properly and precisely to inflict a penalty by a particular precept given to a specified person or persons." [9]

The purpose of this study is to trace the origins of the present penal precept both as a preventive remedy and as a method of procedure for the infliction of a penalty, and

---

6 Instr. *Sacra,* n. 2 — *Codicis Iuris Canonici Fontes,* cura Emi Petri Card. Gasparri editi (9 vols., Romae postae Civitate Vaticana: Typis Polyglottis Vaticanis, 1923-1939) (Vols. VII-IX, ed. cura et studio Emi Iustiniani Card. Serédi.) n. 2005 (hereafter cited as *Fontes); Acta Sanctae Sedis* (41 vols., Romae, 1865-1908), XIII (1880), 324 ff.

7 Inst. *Cum magnopere,* 1883 - *Fontes,* n. 4900; *Collectanea Sacrae Congregationis de Propaganda Fide* (2 vols., Romae: Typographia Polyglotta S. C. de Prop. Fide, 1908), n. 1568.

8 Coronata, *Institutiones Iuris Canonici* (2 ed. 5 vols., Taurini: Marietti, 1939-1947), IV. n. 1816. (Cited hereafter as *Institutiones).*

9 *Institutiones,* III, n. 1453.

then to discuss the law as now contained in the Code of Canon Law.

ARTICLE 1, The Concept of Penal Precept in the *Decretum Gratiani*

In the *Decretum Gratiani* the term precept was not used univocally, and other words were used to convey the same meaning. [10] Nevertheless an attempt was made to distinguish more exactly the difference between precept, counsel and command. Precept implied a grave obligation in conscience, and disobedience to it was regarded as gravely sinful. [11] The scope of precept extended even to what might seem unjust and illicit subject matter. [12] In the use of precept for correction or punishment the ordinary and fundamental norm of issuing admonitions was necessary. [13]

Concerning the subject matter of precepts, the *Decretum* established general outlines of the superior's power. No command of a prelate, contrary to the divine law, should be obeyed, and a sentence of excommunication imposed on a subject who refused to comply with such an evil command was invalid, since such sentence was binding before neither God nor the Church. [14]

Perhaps the closest resemblance to the modern motion of a penal precept appears in the gloss on a canon derived from a letter of Pope Gregory the Great (590-604) to the Bishop of Salona in Dalmatia. [15] Here an excommunication was threatened if the bishop should celebrate the divine mysteries before the question of the lawfulness of his election had been decided by the pope. Since the implication of a precept in this canon is more fully discussed by the Decretalists, the full study of that implication may be deferred. Here it suffices to record two remarks of the glossators

---

10 C. 9, C. XXVIII, 2. 1 - *Decretum Gratiani, emendatum et notationibus illustratum una cum glossis (Romae,* 1583); also C. 25, C. XI, q. 3; Jaffé, *Regesta Pontificium Romanorum ab condita Ecclesia ad annum post Christum natum MXCXVIII* (2 ed., correctam et auctam auspiciis Guglielmi Wattenbach, curaverunt F. Kaltenbrunner (for documents up to the year 590), P. Ewald (for documents from 590 to 882), S. Lowenfeld (for documents from 882 to 1198), 2 vols. in 1, Lipsiae, 1885-1888) n. 1428 (cited hereafter as *Jaffé.)*

11 C. 3. C. XIV, q. 1.

12 C. 5, C. XXIII, q. 1; c. 8, D. C.

13 C. 23, C. XVII, q. 4; Jaffé, n. 2864; Migne, *Patrologia Cursus Completus, Series Latina* (221 vols., Parisiis, 1844-1864), CXIC, 1134 (cited hereafter as MPL).

14 C. 101, C XI, q 3 et Dictum Gratiani, hoc loco.

15 C. 24, D. LXIII; Jaffé, n. 1352.

regarding the penalty. The gloss quoted the opinion of some unnamed commentators, that the words of the canon, *"sub interpositione excommunicationis mandavi si divina celebraret"* levelled an excommunication if this form defined or applied a law. If, on the other hand, the form *constituted* a right, the excommunication was not actually inflicted but simply threatened. The latter position was held by the glossator himself, Ioannes Teutonicus (1245), since "these words do not have the force of a sentence but only of a threat".

The second point regarded the duration of such precept if the death of a superior occurred before the stated conditions were fulfilled. According to the bald statement of the *Glossa Ordinaria,* in such a case the subject incurred the excommunication; "ita aliquis excommunicatur a mortuo". [16]

ARTICLE 2, The Concept of Penal Precept in the Decretals and in the Decretalists

Like the Decree of Gratian, the Decretals lack a full treatment of precept as a separate canonical institute. Hence the doctrine is gleaned principally from the teachings of the glossators.

The subject matter of these precepts was the enforcing or limiting of rights otherwise determined or constituted, as for example the right of a claimant to prosecute the fulfillment of the judgment rendered in his favor, the power of an archbishop to absolve the subjects of his suffragan from an unjust excommunication, while still obliging them under precept to render satisfaction to the suffragan concerning the cause of the excommunication, [17] the warning given to a cleric to resume residence in his benefice, [18] or the command given a community to fulfill its obligation of paying tithes. [19] A precept imposed on a community obliged each member. [20]

16 Glossa ad c 24. D LXIII.

17 C. 8, X, *De officio judicis ordinarii,* I, 31 - *Decretales D. Gregorii Papae IX, una cum Glossis Restitutae,* Romae, 1582; Potthast, *Regesta Pontificium Romanorum inde ab anno post Christum natum MCXCVIII ad annum MCCCIV* (2 vols., Berolini, 1874-1875), n. 250. (Cited hereafter as Potthast.)

18 C. 28, X, *De appellationibus, recusationibus et relationibus,* II, 28; Jaffé, n. 10605.

19 C. 4, X, *De decimis, primitiis et oblationibus,* III, 30; Jaffé, 11660; MPL, CC, 613.

20 C. 7, *De rescriptis,* I, 3; Jaffé, n. 14229.

In imposing a precept there was often an accompanying threat of a penalty for disobedience. Thus the cleric warned to resume residence in his benefice was threatened with loss of the prebend without the right of appeal. [21] A certain cleric absolved from an excommunication incurred through his violence to another cleric was to be made by the one absolving him to swear *("in virtute iuramenti praecipias")* that he would desist from such acts in the future. [22]

Like the Decretists, the Decretalists differed on the nature of the penalty attached to a precept under the forms, *"praecipio sub poena excommunicationis"*, [23] *"sub anathema prohibemus,"* [24] and the form *"sub excommunicationis interpositione mandavi"* which was contained in the canon *Salonitanae* of the Decree of Gratian. [25] The glosses revolved around the nature of the precepts implied here. Bernard of Parma (d. 1266) stated: "If a judge should say I command *(praecipio)* under penalty of excommunication, or I command under threat the excommunication that you perform this act, the subject cantravening this command is not thereby excommunicated." [26]

In his commentary on this canon, Hostiensis (1271) understood such a prohibition as implying either of two possibilities. If the prohibition was contained in a law, it was a threat, but if wrought by a judge *(ab homine)*, it was a penalty actually inflicted *(lata sententia)*. The form used in issuing such a sentence determined its nature either as a threat or penalty. Unless the judge in imposing the sentence intended that it have an immediate effect, it could have only the force of a threat. This intent of the judge could be proved by the witnesses before whom the judge had expressed it. Futhermore, since the matter was one of conscience, the word of the judge though he alone attested to the nature of his intention, had to be believed. [27]

In the *Summa Aurea,* commenting on this same canon, Hostiensis gave an example of circumstances determining

---

21 C. 28, X, *de appellationibus, recusationibus et relationibus,* II, 28.

22 C. 10, *de sententia excommunicationis,* V. 39; Jaffé, n. 13967.

23 *Glossa Ordinaria* ad c. un., X, de sagitariis, V, 15.

24 *Loc. cit.*

25 C. 24, D. LXIII.

26—*Glossa Ordinaria* ad c. un., X, *de sagitariis,* V, 15.

27 Henricus de Segusio (Cardinalis Hostiensis), *Commentaria in Quinque Decretalium Libros* (5 vols., Venetiis, 1581, ad c. un., X, *de sagitariis,* V, 15, cited hereafter as *Commentaria).*

the precept as a penalty and not as a mere threat. If a judge thrice warned a malefactor and then commanded him under penalty of excommunication, in spurning that command the delinquent should regard himself as excommunicated. Other commentators, Hostiensis reported, saw a difference between the precept of a judge under a threat of anathema (which would not be an actual penalty), and the precept as restrictive (which would). [28]

Panormitanus (1386-1453) took issue with this doctrine. Since such excommunications were indefinitely stated, they were but threats, and malefactors were not thereby *ipso facto* excommunicated. Panormitanus labelled the doctrine of Hostiensis doubtful in those circumstances in which the intent of the judge would not be evident. Only when some grave danger to the delinquent were not imminent would Panormitanus give credence to the declaration of the judge that it had been his intention actually to punish a delinquent, and not merely to threaten him. Too facile credence given to the undisputed word of the judge alone would give rise to far greater evils and the prostitution of justice. [29]

In the period of the later decretalists and theologians, it was usual to refer to a particular precept as a *sententia particularis*. Legislation enacted by both Popes Innocent III (1198-1216) and Boniface VIII (1294-1303) restricted the imposition of general or particular sentences of excommunication for future delicts or even for past delicts under the form of a threat if suitable reparation had not been made within a prescribed time. In the sentence itself, the reason for acting contrary to this canon had to be mentioned. [30] The gloss to the Bonifatian decretal made a distinction between statute and sentence. The prohibition enacted in the decretal applied to a sentence such as "I excommunicate T, if he steal."

The legislation of Pope Boniface VIII did not *directly* prohibit such sentences, but it restricted the right of the bishop to legislate by statute to punish crimes committed

---

28 Henricus de Segusio (Cardinalis Hostiensis), *Summa Aurea* (Venetiis, 1570), ad c. un., *de sagitariis*, V, 15.

29 Abbas Panormitanus, (Nicholaus de Tudeschis), *Commentaria in Quinque Libros Decretalium*, (5 vols. in 7, Venetiis, 1588), ad c. un., X, *de sagitariis*, V, 15.

30 C. 21. X. *de sententia excommunicationis*. V, 39; Jaffé n. 17053; Mansi, XXII, 636; C. 5, X, *de sententia excommunicationis, suspensionis et interdicti*, V, 11, in VI°; Bulla *ad explicandos*, 14 Apr. 1246, n. 39; Potthast, n. 12062.

outside his territory in contravention of his laws. The gloss, however, applied the doctrine of Pope Innocent IV's legislation to this provision. [31] Commenting on the decretal *A nobis,* [32] which also prohibited the passing of legislation designed to oblige subjects to the laws and statutes of their territory even when absent from it, Hostiensis referred to this doctrine of Pope Innocent. He added that even though a judge should be punished for not observing this requirement of law, nevertheless in the interim his sentence had to be observed. Panormitanus too agreed to this doctrine. Unless there were some cause at the time of sentence, no sentence of excommunication for future delicts could be inflicted. Yet in the event that such a sentence were imposed, without cause, the sentence was binding.

It remained to the great theologian, Franciscus Suarez (1548-1617), to treat of this question more fully and to lay the foundations for part of the doctrine maintained by subsequent commentators, In his treatise *De Censuris in Communi,* [33] Suarez first discussed the opinions of other commentators on the decretal *A nobis,* namely, that a subject outside his own territory could not be excommunicated by means of a statute. But, on the other hand, a subject could be censured by a sentence. The canonists, wrote Suarez, did not state whether they treated of general or particular sentence. The same reasons were applicable to both. Statutes affected only the territory, but sentences affected the person. Therefore, a subject disobedient to the sentence of a prelate incurred the censure even though he were in another territory. [34]

The general rule governing the issuing of a precept was given as follows:

> "Whenever the superior has the right of power of binding by precept a subject dwelling outside the territory, or of imposing on him either a precept whose obligation endures even though the subject be outside the territory or a precept to be executed outside the territory, then, if a censure

---

31 C. 2, *de constitutionibus,* I 2, in VI°.

32 C. 4, X, *de sententia excommunicationis, suspensionis et interdicti,* V, 39.

33 *De Censuris in Communi,* Disp. V, sect. V, *Opera Omnia* (28 vols., editio a Carolo Berton, Parisiis, 1856-1861). Vol. XXIII, par. 2, (hereafter cited *De Censuris).*

34 *Ibid,* n. 2.

> is legitimately attached to such precept, the censure is incurred whenever the subject violates the precept even outside the territory. The reason is evident. The cause offered for incurring the censure is contumacy and the violation of a precept. In this case the subject wherever he be is contumacious and violates the precept if he does what the precept forbids. Therefore he incurs the censure. If contumacy is supposed according to the tenor of the law, absence alone cannot prevent censure. Nor can the diversity of territory impede the execution if wrought in virtue of the law itself and without external or corporal force which might disturb either the peace or good order." [35]

Furthermore when outside his proper territory a subject could be obliged to the precept of his superior for other reasons such as the good of the subject himself or the fact that the prelate had commanded the subject to observe a precept wherever he might be. This could be enforced even under threat of censure. Thus a bishop could forbid one of his clerics to exercise any clerical functions outside the diocese. In the same way, a religious could be commanded by his provincial to fast once a week under pain of excommunication. The subject would be held to his observance even though he where outside his own province. Thus territorial precept was distinguished from personal precept. Even if in a given province there were a custom or general precept to fast every Friday binding upon every subject even when outside the limits of the province, the subject could not be held to that precept or custom nor would he incur the censure if he violated the custom or precept. It would be otherwise, were the precept imposed directly on a person. [36]

As it is the nature of law to be perpetual, so it is the nature of precept to be transitory and mutable. Personal precept, also called *praeceptum hominis,* falls directly on the person subject to the authority imposing it, and may oblige him even when outside the territory of the superior. [37]

Pirhing (1606-1679) followed the doctrine of Suarez. Directly and immediately, precept extends to the persons

35 *Ibid,* n. 16.
36 *Ibid,* n. 18.
37 Suarez, *De Legibus et Legislatore Deo,* Lib. III, cap. 34.

subject to the authority issuing the precept and "adheres to their bones", obliging them wherever they may be. [38] Passerini (1595-1677) remarked that although the decretal *A nobis* had forbidden sentences of excommunication for futre delicts, *de facto*, both pontiffs and prelates continued the practice. [39]

Benedict XIV (1740-1758) observed that the common opinion of doctors held that one outside the diocese was not bound by its statues. However, on the question of a particular precept, for example to avoid gambling under pain of *ipso facto* excommunication, the censure would be incurred if the precept were violated outside the limits of the diocese. [40]

ARTICLE 3. The Concept of Penal Precept from the Council of Trent to the Promulgation of the Code of Canon Law.

From the Council of Trent (1545-1563), to the promulgation of the Code, the doctrine and usage of penal precept were influenced by two important developments. One was the institution by the Council of Trent itself of a process for the punishment of the occult crimes of clerics, which came to be known as *suspensio ex informata conscientia.* [41] The other was the approbation by the Sacred Congregation of Bishops and Regulars of the practice of ordinaries imposing precepts on clerics and punishing the transgression of such precepts.

Proper discipline had become hindered in consequence of the necessity of proceeding against unworthy persons with all the protracted formalities, solemnities and publicity of a judicial trial.

Section 1. Penal Precept as Developed by the Practice of Local Curias.

During the eighteenth century several decisions on the use of penal precept were rendered by the Sacred Congre-

38 *Jus Canonicum in Quinque Libros Decretalium* (5 vols. in 4, Dilingae, 1674-1678). Lib. I, tit, II, n. 59.

39 *Commentaria in I, II, et II Librum Sexti Decretalium* (Venletiis, 1698), ad. c. 2, *(Ut animarum), de constitutionibus,* 1, 2, in VI°- p. 129.

40 *De Synodo Dioecesana* (2 ed., 2 vols., Parmae, 1764), Lib., XIII, cap. LV, n. 9.

41 Conc. Trident., Sess. XIV, *de ref.*, c. 1; Mansi, III, 357; S. C. de Prop. Fide, Instr., 20 Oct. 1884 — *Fontes*, n. 4907.

gation for Bishops and Regulars. Treating of the discipline of the clergy, they indirectly established a recognized and legally valid procedure thus preparing the way for the Instruction of 1880, which would more formally determine the nature of penal precept when it would provide a summary procedure calculated to safeguard the demands of justice, protect the good name of the clergy and render more easy the maintenance of discipline.

In January, 1712, the Sacred Congregation reviewed the case of a priest of the diocese of Besancon, who had been deprived of his benefice for violating a precept *de non conversando cum quadam muliere*. The Congregation ordered that he was not to be reinstated unless he were given a penal precept in writing enjoining him under grave penalties, even privation of the benefice at the discretion *(tuo arbitrio)* of the dean of the college. [42]

In another case, in September, 1727, the Congregation revoked a like precept imposed on a priest. [43] The facts being insufficient to sustain the precept, the Congregation ordered its revocation and at the same time rebuked the tribunal, warning it to proceed with greater circumspection in similar cases.

A precept *de non conversando* should be preceded by three admonitions. If the precept were ill-founded, the Congregation sternly prescribed that the erring tribunal issue a formal decree attesting to the innocence of the accused in order to undo the prejudice to the person's good name. Thus in September, 1731, all the acts of a process were annulled, and the vicar general [44] of the diocese of Tivoli was commanded to issue a decree attesting the innocence of the accused, a woman. But when the woman requested the decree, a new precept renewing the former was imposed. Thereupon the Sacred Congregation ordered anew the publication of the decree, and demanded that it be notified of the fulfillment of its orders.

Not only should a three-fold admonition procede the infliction of a penal precept but morever caution and prudence should be used lest the reputation of an innocent

42 *Analecta Juris Pontificii* (Romae, 1855-1869; Parisiis, 1872-1891), XIX, (1880), col. 1128 (cited hereafter as *AJP)*.

43 *AJP*, XIX, (1880), col. 1118-1119.

44 *AJP*, XIX (1880), col. 1120-1121.

woman suffer through rash accusation. These were the prescriptions of the Constitution, *"Iustitae gladium"* of Pope Benedict XIV, issued in 1749. [45] Nor should precepts be easily inflicted without sufficient proof. If the acused were proved innocent, the precept had to be revoked entirely.

Similarly, an effort to protect the reputation of the accused was made in a response dated August 28, 1750. If the precept were "paternal" it was to be administered in secret by the bishop personally. No penance might be inflicted and no notation might be made in the register. [46]

In 1838, some indication of the duration of precepts was given, and in the following year, it was repeated. The time was to be determined in the sentence or in the injunction of the precept. If no time were stated, the duration was understood to be one year. [47]

In deciding the case of a laic convicted of rape the Congregation enjoined the bishop to impose a precept *de honeste vivendo.* [48] The sentence imposed for violation of a precept in another case was confirmed and the precepts were to be renewed under pain of even greater penalty. [49] Likewise, the suspension *a divinis* inflicted for disobedience of a precept was upheld and the same precept was to remain in force. [50]

On March 2, 1866, the Sacred Congregation replied to the question submitted by the Procurator General of the Order of Preachers, whether the extrajudicially and orally inflicted suspensión for occult cause by the Master General was valid. The reply was in the affirmative, as long as the precept were given *per modum praecepti particularis.* [51]

Section 2. The Summary Procedure Established in 1880

More than any other part of public law, that which governs criminal law and procedure reflects and is influ-

45 *Collectanea in Usum Secretariae S. C. Episcoporum et Regularium* (ed. A Bizzari, Romae, 1885), (cited hereafter as *Collectanae S. C. Ep. et Reg.)*

46 *AJP,* XIX (1880), col. 1124.

47 *Collectanae S. C. Ep. et Reg.,* p. 193. In a footnote, the editor stated this rule applied to civil tribunals, but that it could also serve as a guide for ecclesiastical courts.

48 *Reatina,* 27 Aug. 1841, *op. cit.,* p. 184.

49 *Ferentina,* 10 mart. 1843, op. cit., p. 184.

50 *Signina,* 2 jan. 1844, op. cit., p. 202.

51 *Collectanea S. C. Ep. et Reg.,* p. 753; *Fontes,* n. 1996.

enced by not only the existing political conditions but also the intellectual and moral developments of the state.[52]

At the time when the Instruction of 1880 was issued, the falling off of the Christian faith together with the separation of Church and State accomplished in the centuries[53] following the Protestant revolution rendered less useful the ordinary judicial means formerly of advantage to the Church in the enforcement of proper discipline. The means remaining within the power of the Church were too ineffectual for maintaining order through the existing judicial procedure.[54]

A procedure destined to preserve the pristine integrity of the members of a society must function efficiently with the first signs of danger.[55] The means instituted to ward off danger or punish transgressions must be proportionate and adapted to the persons, rights and duties involved. Therefore a procedure for discipline of the clergy which would incorporate these features is a necessity.[56]

The old judicial forms for the enforcement of discipline had become excessively complex and inefficient, even to the point of occasioning discredit to the entire canonical procedure in criminal trials. The cumbersome and vexatious forms of Roman Law, the incessant disputes on procedure, and the reversals and long delays on appeals, were the underlying causes of this discredit.[57] The countless formalities

---

52 Droste-Messmer, *Canonical Procedure in Disciplinary and Criminal Causes of Clerics* (New York, 1897), p. 22 (cited hereafter as *Canonical Procedure*).

53 Peries, *La Procedure Canonique Moderne dans les Causes Disciplinaires et Criminelles,* (Paris, 1898), pp. 7-8.

54 *Collectanea S. C. Ep. et Reg.*, instr. 11 iun. 1880—*Fontes,* n. 2005. This instruction was restricted to Italy. On January 14, 1882. the same Congregation extended it to France. In 1883, an Instruction issued by the Sacred Congregation for the Propagation of the Faith for use by the Church in the United States made the same dispositions. Since even the numeration of the paragraphs was similar, hereafter, unless otherwise noted, references to articles within the Instructions will refer to both Instructions that of 1880 and that of 1833. The major distinction between the Instructions was that the one promulgated for the United States constituted the ordinary procedure in summary criminal trials of clerics. Smith (*The New Procedure in Criminal and Disciplinary Causes of Ecclesiastics in the United States* (2 ed., New York, 1888), p. 170, footnote) stated that the original Instruction seemed to follow the model established by the Instruction for the Archdiocese of Prague, 1869. (This work will hereafter be cited Smith, *New Procedure*).

55 Lega, *Praelectiones in Textum Codicis Iuris Canonici, De Iudiciis Ecclesiasticis* (4 vols., Romae, 1896-1901), IV, n. 288 (hereafter cited *De Iudiciis*).

56 Lega, *De Iudiciis,* IV, n. 289.

57 Droste-Messmer, *Canonical Procedure,* p. 26.

conduced only to lengthen the proceedings, furnish numerous grounds for nullity, and to serve chicanery. [58]

The Instruction, according to Droste-Messmer, comprised the most essential rules of canonical procedures which the Roman Congregations had followed for the three previous centuries. It was the development of ecclesiastical discipline and criminal procedure as it progressed in the course of the centuries, formally and explicitly in Italy, substantially in the whole Church. [59]

In brief, the Instruction falls into five main headings: I—The Preamble, the obligation of the ordinary to preserve discipline and harmony; II—The Summary Cognition of Investigation, treating of the administration of monitions and precepts, investigation and gathering of proofs; III—The Judicial Cognition comprised of the indictment and contesting of the alleged charges; IV—The Sentence; and V—The Appeal. Within the first and second sections, namely the preamble and the summary investigation, are contained the parts pertinent to this study.

The remedies which the ordinary possessed fell into two general divisions, either preventive or repressive. Preventive measures were designed to impede the evil, to remove the nettles of scandal and also the voluntary occasions and causes of evil doing. [60] On the other hand, repressive measures followed the delinquency having for their goal the recall the malefactor to a realization and reparation of the effects of his crime. [61]

It was left to the prudence and conscience of the ordinary to determine the means with which to achieve these effects. [62] Chief among the means at the disposal of the ordinary were spiritual retreats, admonitions and precepts. [63]

---

58 *Ibid.*, pp. 89-90.

59 *Canonical Procedure*, pp. 23-24. A writer in the *Analecta Juris Pontificii*, XIX, (1180), col. 1128, cited the case handled in 1712 and reviewed above, as proof that the procedure which employed the use of penal precepts was not wholly Italy's.

60 *Instr.*, art. 2. Cf. S. R. Rotae, *Monitorii et Exercitiorum Spiritualium*, die 13 iul. 1909. Coram R. P. D. M. Lega, *Decano*, Decisio XI, n. 9—S. *Romanae Rotae Decisiones seu Sententiae* quae prodierunt ab anno 1909—(Romae: Typis Polyglottis Vaticanis, 1912—), I, (1909), 99 (hereafter cited S. R. R. Decis.).

61 *Instr.*, art. 2.

62 *Instr.*, art. 3.

63 *Instr.*, art. 4.

It is evident that before an ordinary could inflict any of these penal remedies, he had first to make a summary investigation of the facts which might seem to warrant the use of additional and extraordinary means. As a rule, paternal admonitions and persuasions were to be used before recourse to the harsher means of precept. If a penal precept were inflicted without prior admonitions, the subject would suffer defamation and punishment without a chance of offering the defense to which he was entitled by the natural law. [64] A precept had the strength of a condemnatory sentence passed under a suspensive condition until some future event. [65] Were a number of clerics punished by penal precept, the inevitable revelation or suspicion of wrongdoing would seriously have harmed the honor of the Church itself, a damage difficult to repair. [66]

The examples of precept already given and also the dispositions of the Sacred Congregation of Bishops and Regulars, demonstrate the care which had to be exercised to prevent the harmful spread of knowledge of such penalties having been imposed on clerics. The commentators on the Instruction of 1880 and 1883 were restrained and conservative in their treatment of penal remedies, especially precepts. Use of these remedies tended to become public and thus cast a shadow on the reputation of the cleric on whom any of these remedies may have been imposed. [67] Since a precept was juridical, it could hardly remain secret and so could stain one's reputation. [68] Furthermore, the infliction of a penal precept erects a prejudice in the mind of the judge and of other prudent men. [69]

Penal remedies, even vindictive, consist in a privation of rights. An ordinary, therefore, found it most advantageous either to make a test of preventive measures or to call for a voluntary surrender of rights and the reparation of scandal before he proceeded to a judicial sentence out of

---

64 Rota, *Enchiridion Confessarii et Iudicis Ecclesiastici* (Taurini, 1884), n. 642 (cited hereafter as *Enchiridion.)*

65 Lega, *De Iudiciis*, IV, n. 288.

66 Rota, *op. cit.*, n. 645. *Pierantonelli, Praxis Fori Ecclesiastici ad Praesentem Ecclesiae Conditionem Accommodata* (Romae, 1883), p. 85, (cited hereafter as *Praxis*); Droste-Messmer, *Canonical Procedure*, p. 154.)

67 Lega, *op. cit.*, IV, n. 278.

68 *AJP*, XIX (1880), col. 1118; Droste-Messmer, *Canonical Procedure*, p. 145.

69 Lega, *op. cit.*, IV, n. 278.

condemnation. [70] Grave measures were to be used only for proportionately grave offenses. [71]

The summary criminal trial according to the Instruction of 1880 was invalid if it was instituted after the transgression of a precept which had been levied without previous admonitions and investigation. [72] For the imposition of a preventive precept itself there had to be a certain knowledge of the fact that the cleric was in proximate danger of grave evil if he omitted or neglected a certan thing. Or, for a repressive precept, there had to be evidence of the *corpus delecti* for which the delinquent had to render satisfaction. [73] Nevertheless, occasions might arise when the traditional threefold admonition, reinforced by the Instruction, [74] could be omitted to allow for prompt recourse to sterner measures.

To forestall an imminent and grave danger, it was licit to begin with a precept. "Where there is danger in delay, we recede from the rules of common law." Likewise, whenever it was necessary to arrive at the truth, the necessity of admonitions could be sidestepped as long as there were some indication sufficient to move the judge to act. [75] A precept inflicted without admonition was a grave remedy which denoted contumacy on the part of the delinquent. Therefore, unless there were proof of a delict already committed or one probably about to be committed, a precept could not be inflicted so summarily. [76] The investigation had to produce at least semi-full proof, for example the testimony of one witness, an extrajudicial confession, private writings, flight. [77]

Precept, in general, was defined as a permanent command issued to individuals, or a command issued to the

---

70 *Ibid.*, n. 292.

71 Rota, *Enchiridion*, n. 642.

72 Rota, *op. cit.*, n. 642; *Acta et Decreta Concilii Plenarii Baltimorensis Tertii, A. D. MDCCCLXXXIV* (Baltimorae: John Murphy, 1886), n. 309 (hereafter cited *Acta et Decreta* Balt. III).

73 Rota, *op. cit.*, n. 642; Smith, *New Procedure*, p. 33; Lega, *op. cit.*, IV, n. 288.

74 *Instr.*, art. 6; *Acta et Decreta Balt. III*, n. 309; Smith, *Elements of Ecclesiastical Law*, Vol. II, *Ecclesiastical Trials* (5 ed., New York, 1892), n. 1667 (hereafter cited *Elements)*.

75 Rota, *Enchiridion*, n. 643; Smith, *Elements*, III, n. 1791; Droste-Messmer, *Canonical Procedure*, pp. 81, 144, 148.

76 Lega, *De Iudiciis, IV*, n. 288.

77 Ferraris, *Prompta Bibliotheca Canonica, Iuridica, Moralis, Theologica, necnon Ascetica, Polemica, Rubristica, Historica* (9 vols., Romae, 1885-1899), (s. v. *Probatio*, nn. 13-19). (Cited hereafter as *Prompta Bibliotheca)*.

whole community without perpetuity.[78] A penal precept was an injunction to perform or to omit something under penalty of a delict issued by a judge to one who, after having been warned, was found to be a malefactor after at least a summary investigation.[79] This is essentially the same definition as that presented by Smith "the command of a bishop or judge formally directing a delinquent Ecclesiastic, i. e., one who upon the required previous informal inquiry, has been found guilty of reprehensible conduct and who has been duly warned, to do this or avoid that, on pain of being otherwise visited... with such or such an ecclesiastical punishment."[80]

By command of the ordinary, a precept was to be inflicted in writing by the diocesan curia, that is, by the chancellor in the presence of the Vicar General and two witnesses. It defined what had to be done or avoided, and contained a threat of penalty for the transgression. Violation of such a precept was cause for instituting a summary trial.[81]

In instituting the summary procedure for facilitating disciplinary and criminal process, the Instructions of 1880 and 1883 expressly provided that the essential demands of justice be protected and that canonical uniformity and regularity be preserved.[82] A just summary process included at least the following elements:[83] An informal investigation (arts. 12, 15-21), an informal accusation (arts. 22, 23), citation for trial (art. 14), a contesting of the alleged delict (arts. 26-29), collection and presentation of proofs to the judge (arts. 15, 16, 32), right and presentation of defense (arts. 25, 27, 28, 30-32), the written declaration of sentence (arts. 34, 35).

---

78 Wernz, *Ius Decretalium,* (2. ed., 6 vols., Romae et Prati, 1906-1913), I, n. 135.

79 *Instr.*, art. 5, 6, 7; Rota, *Enchiridion*, n. 642; Wernz, however, defined a canonical admonition as a precept given to a subject by a competent judge who enjoined the subject to do or omit something together with a threat of corresponding penalty in the event of a transgression.—*Ius Decretalium,* VI, n. 255. A decision of the Rota signed by Lega used a like definition. Cf. *S. R. R. Decis.*, I (1909), 99.

80 Smith, *Elements,* III, n. 1787.

81 *Instr.*, art. 10. Smith remarked, however, that one could violate a precept without committing a crime, e. g., a precept to avoid frequenting taverns for an ecclesiastic on the way to becoming a drunkard. Disobedience could be punished even though the ecclesiastic did not become drunk on the occasion of a visit to a tavern.—*New Procedure,* p. 50.

82 Introductions to the Instructions.

83 Smith, *New Procedure,* p. 54.

Great latitude was allowed to the ordinary in the exercise of his discretion not only in the using of penal remedies but also in having recourse to a summary trial itself.[84] In individual cases, "even where the bishop has positive and certain knowledge of a transgression, he is still at liberty, according to his good judgment, prudence and charity, not to proceed at once to a judicial trial, but to try admonitions and salutary precepts." [85] Recourse should first be had to paternal and extrajudicial remedies. If a bishop did not make at least a summary investigation and hear the cleric, he could easily have been lead into error. [86] Even were a crime fully established, as long as the end of the law could be obtained by extrajudicial process, the ordinary should not have recourse to the harsher means of a trial. [87]

An investigation might have revealed only light indications of guilt or perhaps more weighty signs, which however did not provide sufficient proof of a delict or finally, the indications might have been definite enough to give full or at least almost complete proof. Only in the last eventuality could an ordinary order a criminal trial [88] To break the dilemma presented by the obligation to enforce the demands of law on the one hand and those of expediency and prudence on the other, "public welfare takes precedence over the law where its execution would be injurious to society." [89]

Section 3. The Abolition of the Process *ex Notorio*

By the nineteenth century, the ancient criminal process *"ex notorio"* had not only fallen into desuetude but the whole tenor of jurisprudence was decidedly antagonistic to it. Authors leaned heavily to at least recourse to a summary procedure because of the inherent difficulties of the procedure *"ex notorio"* and of the almost inescapable danger of grave injustice.

Thus, commentators reviewed the opposition to the process *"ex notorio"* and showed their own disfavor. Rota's

---

84 *Instr.*, art. 1, 3, 9.

85 Droste-Messmer, *Canonical Procedure*, p. 145.

86 Wernz, *Ius Decretalium*, V, 883.

87 Droste-Messmer, *Canonical Procedure*, p. 80.

88 Andreas B. Meeham, *Compendium Juris Canonici* (Roffal, 1899), p. 243.

89 Instr., art. 3, Droste-Messmer, *Canonical Procedure*, p. 66 and 148; Meehan, *op. cit.*, p. 245; Pierantonelli, *Praxis*, Tit. III, nn. 16, 18, 20.

(1879) condemnation of a proceeding *"sola facti veritate inspecta"* was quoted approvingly by Droste-Messmer (1847-1930) [90] "a kind of trial without any order or form and which canonists call a strange, odious and terrible proceding. It is called a *judicium statarium, ex abrupto, more belli,* and takes place when, on account of the notoriety, atrocity and cruelty of the crime, the judge is content with any solid proof of the fact in order to pronounce sentence at once."

The process *ex notorio* was based on the principle "manifesta accusatione non indigent". [91]

Notoriety arose from isolated occasional or habitual and continuous acts. Only that notoriety which sprang from isolated or widely separated delicts needed the direct accusation of the ordinary process while that which resulted from habitual delicts needed neither judicial procedure nor proof. [92]

Hence it seems that the process *ex notorio* had fallen into disuse before the promulgation of the Code of Canon Law.

---

90 Rota, *Enchiridion,* n. 611; Droste-Messmer, *Canonical Procedure,* p. 89.

91 C. 16. C. II, q. 1. Cf. also c. 15, C. II, q. 1; c. 10, X, *de filis presbyterorum ordinandis vel non,* I, 17; c. 21, X, *de iureiurando,* II, 24; c. 10, X, *de cohabitatione clericorum et mulierum,* III, 2.

92 Cf. Hostiensis, *Commentaria,* Lib. III, tit. 2, cap. 8; Panorimtanus. *Commentaria,* Lib. II, tit. 24, cap. 21; Lib. V, tit. 1, cap. 9; Franciscus Schmalzgrueber, *Jus Ecclesiasticum Universum,* (5 vols. in 12, Romae, 1843-1845), Lib. V, tit. 1, n. 2; Durandus, *Speculum Iuris,* Vol. III. *De Notoriis Criminbus* (Venitiis, 1677), n. 8; Ferraris, *Prompta Bibliotheca,* s. v. *Notarium,* n. 35; Smith, *Elements,* II, 1254, 1256; III, 1791-1792; Smith, *New Procedure,* pp. 35, 43, 58-59; Droste-Messmer, *Canonical Procedure,* pp. 81, 44, 148; Lega, *De Iudiciis,* IV, *Acta Sancta Sedis* (41 Vols., Romae, 1865-1908), Vol. XVIII (1885), 56 ff. (Hereafter cited *ASS*). S. R. Rotae, Pharen. *(Iurium et Poenarium),* 10 inn. 1910 coram R. P. D. Guilelmo Sebastianellii, Dec. XX, n. 7; *S. R. R. Decis.,* II, (1910), 196.)

PART TWO

CANONICAL COMMENTARY

CHAPTER II

THE DEFINITION AND DIVISION OF THE PENAL PRECEPT

It is the right of perfect societies to govern themselves, to define the ends for which they were founded, to determine the means to attain these ends, effectively to propose these means to their members and finally to compel observance of laws properly enacted and promulgated. [1]

The vast and uncodified legislation by which the Church was governed until the present century gave place to the more compact and definitive Code of Canon Law. While putting an end to several old controversies, the present codification did not entirely dispel all the cloudiness, either within points of its own legislation or within common interpretations. As societies go, the Church has almost endless age of experience. Therefore, the judicial wisdom engendered throughout these ages and sharpened through their inevitable conflict and turmoil dictated that provision by which recourse should be had to the older law to explain and interpret and understand the new. [2]

An admirable case in point, to illustrate this evolution, is the particular penal precept. Incorporated into the Code of Canon Law, it did clarify several points previously disputed. Nevertheless, as a legal institute, its formulation is so new that many grave problems have arisen from its very newness and a too summary treatment within the body of the law. Conflicting opinions on both interpretation and application seem able to bolster their theses by reference to parallel passages in the new law, to common sources

---

1 Canon 2214. Cf. Lega-Bartoccetti, *Commentarius*, in *Iudicia Ecclesiastica* (3 vols., Romae: Anonima, Libraria Cattolica Italiana, 1938-1941), III, 151 (hereafter cited as *Commentarius*).

2 Canon 6.

within the old law or to common practice. Indeed the very definitions of the topic are variant. Undoubtedly, dissonance in this so basic chord accounts for the discord of opinions in the dependent questions and conclusions.

ARTICLE 1. The Definition of the Penal Precept

As the term implies, penal precept originates within the power of jurisdiction. The right to issue a penal precept flows from the right of jurisdiction possessed by legitimately constituted authority whose commands are enacted through such various institutes as laws, statutes and precepts. A precept is a command or an injunction which, given by a competent superior, obliges in the external forum.[3] It is evident that a particular penal precept by its very nature pertains to the jurisdiction exercised in the external forum. As it threatens or inflicts a penalty, it is directed towards single individuals. The penal precept, as Roberti says, is like a most particularized or individualized law which in all things is equivalent to a law unless it should appear otherwise from other factors.[4]

By means of a precept, a penalty may be either threaten or inflicted.[5] Thus, a penal precept is either an attempt to effect the correction or break the contumacy of a delinquent and, by threat of penalty, to deter him from a crime which he might otherwise commit, or precept is the actual penalizing *per modum praecepti particularis* of a delinquent for a crime already committed and for which he has been legitimately convicted.[6]

In canon 2306, precept is classified as one of the penal remedies. Though penal remedies have for their purpose to prevent evil, remove the sting of scandal, the voluntary causes and occasion of delinquency[7] nonetheless they have

---

3 Beste, *Introductio in Codicem* (ed. altera, Colleville, Minn.: St. John's Abbey Press, 1944), p. 24 (cited hereafter as *Introductio).*

4 *De Delictis et Poenis* (Vol. I, pars. 1, 1930; Vol. I, pars 2, 1938; Romae apud Aedex Facultatis Iuridicae ad. S. Apollinaris) Vol. I, pars 1, p. 76; Coronata, *Institutiones* III, 379; IV, 108; Sole, *De Delictis et Poenis* (Romae, 1920), p. 102; Noval, *Commentarium Codicis Iuris Canonici, Liber IV, De Processibus,* Pars. I, *De Iudiciis* (Romae: Marietti 1920), n. 755 (cited hereafter as *De Iudiciis);* Lega-Bartoccetti, *Commentarius* III, 195.

5 Canons 2310 and 1933, § 4.

6 Cf. p. 3.

7 Canons 2307-2311, § 1.

a general penal character [8] inasmuch as they lessen the honor of the one on whom they are imposed. [9]

The opportune imposition of a penal remedy, however, serves also to forestall the infliction of more severe penalties. As remedies, these penalties have somewhat of the nature of medicinal penalties even though they can be used on those who are not contumacious and even on those whose delinquency does not appear with certainty. Their principal and immediate end is the correction and amendment of the delinquent or of the one in danger of sinning. [10] However, a precept to which a sanction is attached can also be given to subjects to induce them more efficaciously to the observance of a law or precept. Hence, in a case of this kind, since there is neither correction or recall from some habit of sinning, the precept, though penal has not the proper nature of a penal remedy. [11] Preventive precepts are imposed on those who conduct themselves inordinately, even though they may not be guilty of a true and proper delict, or those who are only the probable or doubtful perpetrators of a delict. [12] Morsdorf [13] considers that only correction and custody (vigilance) possess a truly and specifically genuine penal character. More correctly, Berutti [14] terms precept and vigilance as repressive by nature and correction as either preventive or repressive.

On the other hand, repressive remedies have for their end the reparation of proven crimes. They may also be used to increase a penalty. [15]

As stated previously [16] precept as a preventive remedy is aptly defined as "a command given by a legitimate ecclesiastical superior by which there is accurately indicated what the subject *(praeventus)*, must do or avoid, together with a threat of penalty for transgression". And the cano-

---

8 Canon 2216, § 3.

9 Prümmer, *Manuale Iuris Canonici* (4 et 5 ed. Freiburgi, Brisgoviae: Herder & Co., 1927), p. 671 (cited hereafter as *Manuale)*; Morsdorf, *Rechtsprechung und Verwaltung in Kanonischen Recht* (Freiburgi, Brisgoviae: Herder, 1941), p. 164 (cited hereafter as *Rechtsprechung)*.

10 Berutti, *Institutiones Iuris Canonici*, (5 vols. Taurini: Marietti, 1936-1943), VI, 63 (cited hereafter as *Institutiones)*.

11 *Ibid.*, pp. 242-243.

12 *Ibid.*, p. 238.

13 *Rechtsprechung*, p. 164.

14 *Op. cit.*, VI, 238.

15 Canon 2311, § 1.

16 p. 2.

nical procedure of inflicting a penalty by means of precept is aptly described in these words: "To inflict a penalty after the manner of a precept is the same as to inflict a penalty not enacted in any law or general precept but properly and precisely to inflict a penalty by means of a particular precept given to a specified person or persons." [17]

ARTICLE 2. The Form of the Penal Precept

The legislation which governs the forms of precepts is contained in canons 24 and 2225. The latter treats of the execution of a precept already given while the former treats of the mode of imposing the precept. [18] The difference, in Coronata's opinion, [19] is that the precept treated in canon 24 is judicial, and that in canon 2225 is extrajudicial.

> Canon 24 states: *"Praecepta, singulis data, eos quibus dantur, ubique urgent, sed iudicialiter urgeri nequeunt et cessant resoluto iure praecipientis, nisi per legitimum documentum aut coram duobus testibus imposita fuerint"*.

> Canon 2225 employs very similar wording: *"...si vero poena latae vel ferendae sententiae inflicta sit ad modum praecepti particularis, scripto aut coram duobus testibus ordinarie declaretur vel irrogetur, indicatis poenae causis, salvo praescripto canonis* 2193". [20]

Since there must be legal proof of the action of the superior in the issuance of precepts, the Code rightly determines what form such acts must take. [21] A precept issued in either of the forms here mentioned may be classified as formal: those which do not follow these forms

---

17 Coronata, *Institutiones,* III, 378. Authors do not always use the term precept in either of these proper and restricted senses. For example, Roberti (*De Delictis et Poenis,* I, 77) confuses admonition as a penal remedy (Canons 2307-2310) with admonition which is an attempt to break contumacy (canons 2233, 2 and 2242, 2). Roberti terms the latter an admonition containing a precept or even a "true and proper penal precept". Cf. also Prümmer, *Manuale,* p. 672; Wernz-Vidal, *Ius Canonicum* (7 vols. in 8, Vol. VII, Romae, Apud Aedes Universitatis Gregorianae: 1937) VII, 32; Lega-Bartoccetti, *Commentarius,* III, 194; Van Hove, *De Legibus Ecclesiasticis* (Mechliniae: H. Dessain, 1930), p. 361.

18 Lega-Bartoccetl, *Commentarius,* III, 195.

19 *Institutiones,* IV, 108.

20 Canon 2193 leaves it to the prudent judgment of the ordinary to disclose to the culprit the reasons for his suspension *ex informata conscientia.*

21 Ayrhinac-Lydon, *Penal Legislation in the Code of Canon Law,* (revised edition, New York: Benziger Brothers, 1944), p. 37 (cited hereafter as *Penal Legislation).*

may be termed informal. Regarding formal precepts, neither canon 24 nor canon 2225 fully determines what is meant by legitimate document. Futhermore, the latter canon uses the word *ordinarie,* which leaves it to the prudent judgment of the superior to determine whether in a special case and for grave reasons this formality may be omitted.[22]

In the usual case the precept should be so drawn up that its authenticity may be evident, for example through signature and seal.[23] The document may be either public or private according to the norms established in canon 1813.[24] In Coronata's opinion,[25] a notarized document or one issued according to the norms established in canon 2308 would be sufficient.[26] A simple letter of the ordinary would suffice if it could be proved that the letter itself was legitimately conveyed either through courier, publication, or other legitimate modes, or for example by the signature of the subject on the letter or postal receipt.[27]

Woywod[28] agreed that a simple letter properly dated and addressed would be sufficient to serve as a formal precept. It should, however, also express the wish of the ordinary to use his power of issuing a precept according to the canons. This precept would be judicially enforceable.

According to Blat, Article 8 of the Instruction of 1880 has not been abrogated by the Code.[29] This formulated the procedure for conveying a precept to a delinquent. The precept was to be imposed by the chancellor before the vicar general or two witnesses, clerical or lay. The acts were to be signed by these parties and the subject (prae-

22 Coronata, *Institutiones,* III, p. 347, note 4.

23 Vermeesch-Creusen, *Epitome Iuris Canonici,* (6. ed., 3 vols., *Mechliniae:* H. Dessain, 1937-1946), I, 129 (cited hereafter as *Epitome*).

24 Lega-Bartoccetti, *Commentarius,* III, 196.

25 Institutiones, I, 51.

26 *"Si ex alicuius conversatione scandalum vel gravis ordinis perturbatio oriantur, est locus correptioni, ab Ordinario per se vel per interpositam personam, etiam per epistolam faciendae, peculiaribus accommodatae conditionibus personae et facti de quo agitur."*

27 Coronata, *Institutiones,* I, 51; et IV, 109. Cf. also canon 2309, 5. Van Hove holds that a simple letter would not suffice. *De Legibus Ecclesiasticis,* p. 367.

28 *A Practical Commentary on the Code of Canon Law* (revised edition by Callistus Smith, 2 vols. New York: Joseph F. Wagner, 1946), I, 16 (cited hereafter as *Commentary*). Cf. also Coronata, *Institutiones,* IV, 109, text and note 6.

29 *Commentarium Textus Codicis Iuris Canonici,* Liber V, *De Delictis et Poenis* (Romae: Collegio "Angelico" 1924), p. 192 (hereafter cited as *Commentarium*). Cf. also Lega-Bartocetti, *loc. cit.*

ventus) if he so willed. Finally, the vicar general was empowered to impose an oath of secrecy on all concerned. However, no indication of these formalities is contained in the Code and therefore the officials named are not necessary to the procedure. The ordinary would be able to impose the oath of secrecy since it seems that this provision proceeds from an attempt to protect the right to good repute.

It would be helpful, of course, to obtain the signature of the subject to the precept given him; but if he refuse, then a notarized or witnessed document would be necessary. The public good requires that the form should not be easily dispensed with. The form set forth in canon 2225 does not exclude the exceptional case in which neither form, document or witnesses is required. Evidently these forms are not required for validity. [30] If the precept be adminstered orally, it should be reduced to writing by the notary, signed by the ordinary and also by the subject if he so wish.

While the regular form is required simply for licitness, the motives which inspire the precept must be expressed for validity. [31] In the case of censures, the reasons are absolutely required for validity, since censures presume contumacy which cannot be proved without admonitions.

In respect to the document itself, in a penal precept the form should express the substantial elements of the matter. In canon 2310 there is some indication of the form of a preventive precept. It should state what should be done or avoided by the subject, and should threaten some penalty even though indeterminate.

The repressive precept which inflicts the threatened penalty should be slightly different in form, since its purpose is different. Muñiz [32] offers a complete and accurate form for the written document. It should express: (1) the authority of the superior inflicting the precept; (2) the subject; (3) the penalty inflicted; (4) the cause or delict;

---

30 Roberti, *De Delictis et Poenis*, Vol. I, pars. 2, pp. 299-300; Wernz-Vidal, *Ius Canonicum*, VII, 204.

31 Heylen, *De Censuris*, (4 ed. Mechliniae: H. Dessain, 1945), p. 39; Coronata, *Institutiones*, IV, 109.

32 *Procedimientos Eclesiasticos*, (2. ed. 3 vols., Sevilla Imp. y Lib. de Sabaino de Izquierdo, 1925), III, 559 (cited hereafter as *Procedimientos*). Cf. also Roberti, *De Delictis et Poenis*, Vol. I, pars. 2, p. 299; Cocchi, *Commentarium in Codicem Juris Canonici*, (8 Vols. in 5, V. ed., Taurinorum Augustae, 1938) V. 63. (Cited hereafter as *Commentarium*).

(5) the date, place and seal, the signatures of the ordinary and chancellor or notary, or witnesses. An authentic copy is given or sent to the subject by the chancellor, dean, cursor or by registered mail (with request for return receipt, of course) or finally by publication on the bulletin board of the curia.

The precept may be oral [33] and later reduced to writing. In both the oral and written forms, the causes for the issuance of the precept should be given, since the inferior has the right to know the reason for the punishment. [34] It is a well established custom among civil societies to give the reason for the punishment of members. The exposition of the reason for a .punishment provides an opportunity for proper defense and explanation should the matter be contested. [35] In setting forth the cause of the precept, i. e., the delict, the precept should accurately name the accused, the crime and its circumstances together with the reasons for the decision *in iure et in facto.* Wernz-Vidal suggest that the indication of the cause serves to show to the accsed the way or grounds for recourse. It would also serve to supply for defects of the process should private certitude lack a real fundament. [36] This seems to stretch matters too far for it will be seen later that the procedure by way of precept calls for certitude.

Except canon 2225, the canons which establish a form for precept seem to allow no leeway for informal precepts. Canon 2310 does not give a form for the preventive penal precept. Canon 2225 covers the infliction of penalties by means of the repressive penal precept. Canon 24 is a general canon governing precept and concerns administrative and gubernative precepts. It does not cover penal precept, for by canon 2310 a penal precept must contain a threat of punishment. Canon 24, howver, governs precepts which may be judicially enforced and therefore it requires a definite and exact form.

Though the Code does not mention informal precepts, some authors strive to include them within the ambit of

---

33 *Collectanea S. C. Ep. et Reg.,* p. 193; *Fontes,* n. 1996; Berutti, *Institutiones,* VI, 83; Blat, *De Delictis et Poenis,* p. 65.

34 Ayrhinac-Lydon, *Penal Legislation,* p. 37.

35 Lega-Bartoccetti, *Commentarius,* III, 198; Morsdorf, *Rechtsprechung,* p. 167.

36 *Ius Canonicum,* VII, 204.

penal precepts and to endow them with something of a coercive nature. Informal precepts cannot be judicially enforced. According to the viewpoint of these authors, they do have a certain validity in the internal and external forums. [37] The discussion of the kind of enforcement by which such informal precepts may be urged must be deferred to Chapter V on THE PENALTIES WHICH MAY BE INFLICTED EXTRAJUDICIALLY BY WAY OF PRECEPT.

Two witnesses are sufficient to attest to the legal issuing of a penal precept except in the extraordinary case for which canon 2225 makes provision. Hence, the greater leeway regarding the form of precept applies to the witnesses as well as to the constitution of the document. [38] Therefore, one qualified witness [39] for example, the vicar general, chancellor or notary [40] would suffice to prove either the imposition of a preventive or repressive precept or the infliction of a penalty by a repressive precept. The witnesses are required not only for the solemnity of the act but also with a view to furnishing proof of the imposition of the precept or of the infliction of the penalty. The ordinary rules for the credibility of witnesses [41] an their suitability [42] apply to the witnesses of precept. [43]

ARTICLE 3. The Subject Matter of Penal Precept

The power to use precepts is derived from the general legislative and coercive powers of ecclesiastical superiors. [44] It goes without saying while the subject matter encompassed by precept is wider than that of law, it must possess several like qualities. Law is primarily ordained for the good of society as a whole and does not seek to govern every individual act or to punish every transgression. Precept, on the other hand, while also seeking the common good, is more fittingly suited to the individual subject and the par-

---

37 Cicognani, *Canon Law* (English version by J. O'Hara and F. Brennan, 2nd revised ed., Westminster, Md., Newman Bookshop, 1946), p. 638; Wernz-Vidal, *Ius Canonicum*, I, 265; Coronata, *Institutiones*, IV, 108, note 6.

38 Cf. Page

39 Canon 1791, 1.

40 Canon 1813, 1, 1°, 2°.

41 Canon 1791, § 2.

42 Canons 1856-1758.

43 Van Hove, *De Legibus Ecclesiasticis, p. 368;* Coronata, *Institutiones*, I, 58; Cicognani, *Canon Law*, pp. 637-638.

44 Canons 2220, § 1; 501, § 1; 2310.

ticular evil. Yet, precept ultimately affects the common good as well as the individual good. [45]

Anything contained in the divine, natural or ecclesiastical laws is fit subject matter for precept. A precept may be imposed even when there is only slight suspicion or danger of wrong-doing. Then, too, the general law does not cover every evil but only the common and more serious crimes. By precept, however, an individual may be restrained from crimes not covered by the common law, e. g. fornication. The opportune use of precept serves as a penal remedy to forestall serious delinquency. De Meester [46] rightly considers precept as applicable to the lighter transgressions in which clerics fall from uprightness of life or neglect the obligations of their office, and to the trespasses which enervate ecclesiastical discipline, cause scandal and lead to crime. [47]

Canon 2222, § 1 endows the superior with the faculty of inflicting a penalty for the volation of a law to which there is not attached any sanction. It seems a valid extension within the mind of the legislator to say that the transgression of a precept to which the superior has not attached a sanction can likewise be punished in virtue of this canon when the violation of the precept be scandalous or of special gravity. [48]

It is evident that the subject matter of a precept must be just, honorable, i. e. fitting and proper, and possible of

---

45 Onclin, *De Territoriali vel Personali Legis Indole* (Gemblaci: J. Duculat, 1938), p. 363.

46 *Juris Canonici et Juris Canonico — Civilis Compendium*, (3 vols. in 4, nova ed., Brugis, Desclee de Braumer et sii, 1921-1928) Vol. III, pars 2, p. 228.

47 Though precept can be imposed on *all* subjects, at the present time it is used largely for maintaining clerical discipline.

48 Noval, "De ratione corrigendi et puniendi sive in iudicio sive extra iudicium iure Codicis I. C.", *Jus Pontificium* (Romae, 1921-1940), II (1922). 154. (Cited hereafter as "De ratione corrigendi"-*JP*). Although canon 2222, § 1 treats of violation of laws and not of precept, the latter would seem to be included in this extraordinary provision. The same reason which demands a penalty for specially grave or scandalous violations of law to which there is no penalty attached applies also to precept. Thus this canon may be said to constitute a general warning of penalty for violations of laws or precepts and the conflict between canons 2222, § 1 and 2219, § 3 is appreciably lessened. Cf. also the admirable study on this subject Casey, *A Study of Canon 2222, § 1* (The Catholic University of America Canon Law Studies, N. 290, The Catholic University of America Press, Washington, D. C., 1949), Chapter 7, article III.

achievement. [49] The determination of what constitutes the proper subject matter in a particular case pertains to the superior. He may attach a penalty by way of precept to the divine, natural, and ecclesiastical laws according to the limits of his jurisdiction. He may also attach a sanction to his own legitimate commands. [50] Any inordinate conduct is suitable matter for a preventive precept. [51] The superior may oblige the subject to place an act required by law even though the subject may not agree with the superior's interpretation or seeming extension of the law. The act of the superior in such circumstance may be only the more explicit determination of the law. Likewise the superior may oblige the subject to omit an act which the inferior may not judge to be prohibited by the law. If a law is without sanction in the Code, the superior acts justly and within his jurisdiction when he attaches a sanction to it by means of precept.

ARTICLE 4: The Duration of a Particular Penal Precept

The Code does not speak in any place of the duration of penal precept and as a consequence the duration of a precept must be gauged from other sources. Canon 24 gives a general rule for all precepts. Formal precepts endure even beyond the expiration or suspension of the powers of the superior inflicting them. Informal precepts, however, cease with the expiration of the office of the superior and are suspended with the suspension of his powers. Van Hove considers it necessary that all penal precepts be constructed in the solemn form. [52]

Since preventive precepts circumscribe an individual's rights by adding sanctions to the common law and by defining obligations and duties in finer detail, it seems that they should not be extended beyond the needs of the particular case. As penal remedies they are ordained to prevent an imminent evil or to remove the voluntary occasions of sin. When these ends have been attained, there is no further

---

49 Cocchi, *Commentarium* I, 208. Maroto, *Institutiones Iuris Canonici ad Normam Novi Codicis*, (2 Vols.), Matriti (Madrid) (1919), I, 289. (Cited hereafter as *Institutiones*).

50 Chelodi-Ciprotti, *Ius Canonicum, De Delictis et Poenis* (5th ed., Vicenza: Societa Anonima Typografica, 1943) p. 29. (Cited hereafter as *De Delictis et Poenis*).

51 Berutti, *Institutiones, VI, 238.*

52 *De Legibus Ecclesiasticis,* p. 371.

need of the preventive precept in the usual case. Furthermore, precepts are distinguished from law by duration: precepts are temporary while law is by nature perpetual. Therefore it seems incorrect to consider precept as a penal remedy as perpetual. Coronata appears to be far too rigorous and much too inexact when he states that penal remedies are not removed by absolution or dispensation and are therefore perpetual. [53] There is no valid reason why an ordinary who imposed a preventive precept cannot also remove it. If, for example, a cleric had been given a precept to abstain absolutely from all alcoholic beverages because of the extremes to which the cleric had gone, the ordinary could remove such precept either for a time or entirely when it appeared that the cleric had regained sufficient strength in the virtue of temperance. The question varies, of course, with the individual precept, for example, a precept *de non conversando cum quadam muliere.* In the imposing of a preventive precept the superior may indicate the time for which it is to perdure. If there be no mention of the time, the pre-Code rule seems applicable, that is, such a precept was understood as given for one year. [54] If the matter of the precept be transitory then the term of one year is surely pertinent. [55] Of course the superior could expressly impose a precept *ad beneplacitum nostrum* or *in perpetuum* or for a definite time either longer or shorter than one year. [56]

Repressive precepts are either medicinal or vindicative and are therefore governed by the proper rules concerning these penalties.

---

53 *Institutiones*, IV, 77.

54 *Collectanea S. C. Ep. et Reg.*, p. 193.

55 Maroto, *Institutiones*, I, 296.

56 *Ibid.*

CHAPTER III

THE NATURE OF THE EXTRAJUDICIAL PROCESS IN GENERAL

ARTICLE 1: Comparison with the Judicial Process

The end of the Church is the sanctification of the faithful and, in a special way, of the clergy since it is so intimately connected with the general sanctification of society. The maternal solicitude of the Church, stirred by any imperiling of the sanctity of the clergy consequent upon any loosening of discipline, hastens to drive off the danger. This ecclesiastical solicitude for maintaining or restoring discipline is twofold: first, to prevent the laity from being scandalized by its leaders, and secondly, to procure the edification of the faithful through the working of penance. [1]

By its nature the general legislation on criminal procedure applies to both clergy and laity. The forms of criminal procedure are either ordinary or extraordinary. Thus, in canon 1933 the legislator determines that some delicts are punishable through a trial, while some may be punished extrajudicially. [2] The criminal procedure outlined in canons 1933 and following is the ordinary procedure to be followed in the investigation and determination of a crime, its punishment, the correction of the delinquent and the restoration of good order. [3]

The extraordinary processes are of several types, each calculated to overcome efficiently the peculiar difficulties usually concomitant with attempts at punishing certain delicts. They are summary methods ordained to preserve the essential demands of justice and nevertheless to deal with crime or negligence quickly, economically and with the least possible external agitation and disturbance. An extrajudicial procedure is based on knowledge gained ac-

---

1 Lega, *De Judiciis*, IV, 278, Lega-Bartoccetti, *Commentarius*, III, 153.

2 Noval, "De ratione corrigendi", *JP*, I-II (1921-1922), 155 and III (1923), 204. There are four opinions concerning this canon. They will be discused in Chapter IV.

3 Wernz-Vidal, *Ius Canonicum*, VII, 202: Vermersch-Creusen, *Epitome*, III, 130; Noval, *De Judiciis*, p. 495.

cording to its own proper manner and which takes the place of the knowledge gained by means of a judicial procedure. It also supplants the judgment according to the common law. [4] It is a quick procedure to protect the community from lawbreakers. This is the intrinsic justification for the substitute and summary process. [5]

The Instruction of 1880, having reviewed the deficiencies of the then extant means for maintaining discipline and punishing transgressions, reminded ordinaries of their primary office and duty to prevent and eliminate disorders by means of an opportune and timely recourse to penal remedies. The criminal procedure outlined in the Instruction was incorporated into the Code of Canon Law in Book IV, part I, title XIX. Although the Code has not introduced a new discipline in many matters, it has constituted a discipline with new and certain limits. The necessity of recourse to a criminal trial is reduced to more restricted limits. [6]

In regard to penal precept, however, the present legislation is so general, so cursory, so obscure that authors lament the fact and desire authentic clarification and instruction from the Commission for the Authentic Interpretation of the Code. "It is lamentable," Roberti says boldly, "that the Code should have so obscurely determined the penalties to be inflicted after the manner of a precept. What has been hithertofore neglected can be done by authentic declaration." [7] To which Coronata adds: "If such declaration should come, it would solve an objective doubt and be equivalent to a new law." [8] It is hardly surprising, therefore, to find such widely opposed opinions among the authors, not only about the basic concept of penal precept itself, but also and as a consequence about the interpretation of the canons and parallel passages which govern this institute.

A concept of the nature of the extrajudicial process and a general view of what penalties fall under its scope can be gained only by indirection, that is, first by examining

---

4 Morsdorf, *Rechtsprechung*, p. 159.

5 *Ibid.*, p. 164.

6 Lega-Bartoccetti, *Commentarius*, III, 172.

7 *De Delictis et Poenis*, Vol. I, pars 2, p. 300; "Quaenam poenae applicari possint per modum praecepti", - *Apollinaris* IV (1930), 296 ff. (cited hereafter as "Quaenam poenae" - *Apollinaris*).

8 *Institutiones*, III, 379, note 3.

the judicial process and then by excluding those penalties which are not encompassed by the extrajudicial process *"ad modum praecepti."*

Canon 1552 § 1, states that "by the term ecclesiastical process (or trial) is understood the legitimate discussion and definition of a controversy before an ecclesiastical tribunal in a matter in which the Chuch has the right of judgment." The object of a criminal trial is defined in the same canon. [9] as "delicts with a view to inflicting or declaring a penalty." These elements were united in one definition by Noval, [10] "the legitimate discussion and definition before an ecclesiastical tribunal or a controversy in a criminal matter or concerning a delict, its author and the relative penalty in those things in which the Church has the right of judgment." The same author outlined the remote objects of criminal trials as either condemnatory of declaratory. [11] A condemnatory judgment is "instituted to issue a condemnatory sentence which, besides the cognition of a criminal fact and its author, carries with it either the determination of a penalty not previously determined in the law or precept or the application of a penalty so determined in the law or precept." On the other hand, the declaratory judgment is "instituted to issue a declaratory sentence, that is, one which declares the fact to be certain and criminal, its author as really guilty and the penalty either *a iure or ab homine,* to have been *ipso facto* and certainly incurred."

Although the legislator has provided both judicial and extrajudicial procedures, his desire seems to be that regularly penalties be inflicted through the formal and ordinary process of a trial. [12] In general, the Church abhors arbitrariness and demands a disciplined order in all things. [13]

The formalities of a trial are ordained to safeguard the natural rights of freedom and good repute. No one should

---

9 § 2, 2º.

10 *De Judiciis,* p. 480. Objectively a judgment is, according to Lega-Bartoccetti, *"complexus actorum certo ordine et forma, vi legum determinatarum, quibus iudices competentes et instantiam legitimi actoris cognoscunt de criminibus eorumque auctoribus ut criminosi homines debitas luant poenas." Commentarius*-III, 152.

11 *Op. cit.*, p. 485.

12 Noval, "De ratione corrigendi," *JP*, III (1923), 204; Sipos, *Enchiridion Iuris Canonici* (Pécs; Ex Typographia "Halodas R. T.", 1926) p. 869 (cited hereafter as *Enchiridion).*

13 S. R. Rota, *Pharen.* (Jurium et Poenarum), 29 iul. 1909, coram R. P. D. Aloisio Sincero, Dec. XIII—S. R. R. Decis, I (1909), 110-122.

be condemned unless it be clearly proved that he knowingly, willingly and freely transgressed the rights of society. The general principles of canon law which define a delict, and determine the extent of responsibility are evidences of the Church's desire to safeguard these rights. Through its institution of various modes of procedure and appeal or recourse, it seeks further to defend these natural rights. The proper administration of criminal justice demands that crimes be definitely proved. Private certitude generally does not suffice. Juridical certitude is required. To this end judicial processes are instituted. [14] If, despite discussions, hearings, allegations and accusations of the plaintiff or the promoter of justice, the excuses and defenses of the accused and his advocate along with the observance of all other rigid legal norms, it is not easy to define a delict *in concreto* and to determine the proportionate penalty then without any doubt it will be difficult to define and determine a delict extrajudicially. [15]

The infliction of a penalty as a restriction of rights is odious and cannot be made unless its reasonable basis sufficiently appear in individual cases, that is, only after the cause of the penalty (the delict), its perpetrator and his imputablility, the proportion of the penalty and the hope of achieving the goal of the condemnation or declaration are well established. Regularly these things do not effectively stand forth unless the delict and the penalty are discussed in strict judicial debate. [16] It is true that the law gives to superiors the right to inflict penalties either judicially or extrajudicially but only when they observe the requirements of law by not exceeding the limits of their jurisdiction and by not inflicting certain penalties without regard to the proper procedure for the particular case. [17]

The law makes adequate provisions for exceptional cases, extraordinary circumstances or contingencies. It should be noted, however, that the law gives no general administrative procedure but only particular ones. These may be divided into three types: (a) a special manner of proceeding in penal matters according to canon 1933, § 4

14 Wernz-Vidal, *Ius Canonicum*. VII, 202; Morsdorf, *Rechtsprechung*, p. 116.

15 Noval, "De ratione corrigendi", *JP*, III (1923), 205.

16 Noval, *ibid.*, p. 204.

17 Berutti, *Institutiones*, VI, 82. Cf. also the Instruction of the S. C. de Prop. Fide, 26 Aug. 1775 - *Fontes*, n. 4568.

and canon 2225; (b) and (c) the procedures relative to public order or removal from office according to canons 2168-2195.

ARTICLE 2. General Norms for the Extrajudicial Process by Way of Precept

The ordinary process through a criminal trial is calculated to care for ordinary cases. Special considerations and a desire to institute a quick and easy form for maintaining discipline have induced the introduction of an extrajudicial criminal process by way of precept. Since the legislator has treated the matter of precept so cursorily, the commentators have striven to complete the understanding of the nature and scope of this procedure. Unfortunately, however, the opinions of the commentators are not unanimous even on the essential points of this procedure and their individual treatments are often sketchy and incomplete. "This is indeed unfortunate," Lega-Bartoccetti states, "not only because the law itself is so brief, but also because the opinions of canonists weigh so heavily in penal matters." [18]

The necessity or usefulness of an extrajudicial procedure is indisputable, although individual authors may differently conceive the nature of an extrajudicial procedure in its practical application. [19] Perhaps the only attempt to give a complete though brief picture of what is encompassed by the extrajudicial process by way of precept was that of Noval in an article entitled "De ratione corrigendi et puniendi sive iudicio sive extra iudicium iure Codicis I. C.",

---

18 *Commentarius,* III, 172.

19 Before the publication of the Code of Canon Law, "judiciary order, even in criminal matters, was so complicated with solemnities which had to be observed in substance that they rendered the administration of justice ineffectual. Experience had shown that in order to flee the protracted solemnities of the trial, judges had too easily classified as notorious what really called for judicial proof. The summary process could be observed in those things which were called notorious and hence the process *ex notorio* happily fell into disuse." - Lega-Bartoccetti, *Commentarius,* III, 170-171.

For his part, Rainer seems to err when he states that the former process *ex notorio* can be used at the present time. Admitting that the Code takes no cognizance of such a procedure, he claims it is not wanting in legal value, since in pre-Code times notorious crimes could be penalized without the ordinary judicial formality. In his opinion, this suffices to render the legal practice legitimate in view of canon 6. To substantiate this doctrine, Rainer cites only Ioannes Anderae Barbosa and Wernz but overlooked more modern authors. Therefore it seems warranted to regard his opinion as not sustainable. Cf. Rainer, *Suspension of Clerics* (Catholic University of America Canon Law Studies, No. 111 Washington, D. C., 1937), pp. 152-153; 163. (Cited hereafter as *Suspension).* Cf. also Prümer, *Manuale,* p. 648.

which appeared in several parts in the *Jus Pontificium* for the years 1922-1923. Some other commentators who treated the matter less extensively concede to Noval's opinion the encomium of being the best and strictest interpretation of this process, even though they may disagree wholly or partially with his restrictions. [20] The discussion of the different opinions must be deferred to Chapter IV. The present matter is the extrajudicial process in general.

It belongs to the ordinary to determine when there is need for the judicial process to punish a public delict. [21] This determination must be based on several factors. Thus the delict may not be known as to the fact or it may be know to a few whose character and dispositions offer firm assurance that it would never be revealed. It may, on the other hand, be known or divulged as to fact but its imputability may be known by a few who will not reveal the information. In these cases, according to Noval, [22] the ordinary should proceed to the imposition of secret penal remedies, [23] or to public penal remedies after an extrajudicial confession or conviction; to censures; [24] to suspension *ex informata* conscientia; to any just penalty under canon 2222, § 1; to a penalty according to one of the summary processes; [25] to the expulsion from a religious order; [26] to the denial of promotion to Orders; [27] to the denial of dimissorials; [28] to the general gubernative provisions of canons 2222, § 2 and 1340, §§ 2 and 3; and finally to the special inquisition into the alleged delictual facts with a view to prosecution in the judicial forum.

Recourse to the extrajudicial procedure may be proper in a case in which the judicial procedure is not absolutely necessary to discover the delict and its perpetrator. [29] If the judicial order had to be observed without exception, the eternal salvation of souls, either that of the delinquent or

---

20 E. g., Roberti, *De Delictis et Poenis*, Vol. I pars 2, p. 293 ff.; cf. also Coronata, *Institutiones*, III, 378.

21 Canon 1933, § 1, and 1947.

22 *De Iudiciis*, p. 496; "De ratione corrigendi", *JP*, III (1923); 206.

23 Canon 2309, § 5.

24 Canons 2220, § 1, and 2221.

25 Canons 2168-2185.

26 Canons 653 and 646.

27 Canons 970 and 2222, § 2.

28 Canons 958 and 964.

29 Lega-Bartoccetti, *Commentarius*, III, 189.

of others, which is the ultimate end of a penalty would be frustrated. Regularly, however, the judicial process is to be observed, unless because of the contingencies envisioned in canon 2193, § 3 it becomes impossible to follow the full legal formalities. [30] The judgment on this is committed to the prudence of the ordinary. [31] Cappello [32] states that when a judicial process would be impossible, wholly useless or even harmful to the good of souls by reason of scandal or damage derived from a trial or in view of the peculiarities of persons concerned or of attendant circumstances, a penalty can be inflicted extrajudicialy after the manner of precept.

Thus, while paragraph 4 of canon 1933 [33] may seem to be an exception to the general rule of paragraph 1, [34] it must be observed that only certain or incontestable delicts can be punished without a trial and then only according to a special extrajudicial process. Thus, when a superior acting in his capacity of legislator, establishes a law or precept, he can and does constitute a penalty extrajudicially when be states in the law or precept, that the penalty will be incurred *ipso facto*. It seems, from the sense of canon 2225, that all penalties other than those issued after the manner of a particular precept must be inflicted through the ordinary process. [35]

Paragraph 4 of canon 1933 does not actually contain an exception to the general rule on the obligation of conducting a formal trial for public delicts. The legislator here treats not of delicts in violation of the law but of delicts which consist in violation of the particular precept given on the occasion of the previous violation of a law not strengthened by any sanction or even of one so strengthened but for whose correction and punishment it may be morally impossible to institute a trial and yet which ought to be punished. [36]

---

30 Berutti, *Institutiones*, VI, 82.

31 Canon 2223, § 4. The canon directly concerns the declaration of a *latae sententiae* penalty, but should likewise be understood as the infliction of a penalty. - Noval, "De ratione corrigendi", *JP*, II (1922), 149.

32 "Irrogatio poenae per modum praecepti particularis", *Periodica*, XIX (1930), 36*-38*.

33 *"Poenitentia, remedium poenale, excommunicatio, suspensio, interdictum, dummodo delictum certum sit, infligi possunt etiam per modum praecepti extra iudicium."*

34 *"Delicta quae cadunt sub criminali indicio sunt delicta publica."*

35 Noval, *De Iudiciis*, p. 495.

36 Noval, "De ratione corrigendi", *JP*, II (1922), 154.

The usefulness of an extrajudicial procedure is also seen from the provision made by the law in canon 2222, § 1, "Although a law have no sanction attached, the legitimate superior can punish its transgression with some just penalty even without previous threat of penalty, if the grave scandal given or the special gravity of the transgression make such action feasible; otherwise a delinquent cannot be punished unless he had been first admonished with a threat of either a *latae* or a *ferendae sententiae* penalty in the event of transgression, and he nevertheless shall have violated the law." [37] Both the good of the delinquent and the public good demand that a penalty be inflicted on him publicly and promptly. [38] It should be noted, however, that canon 2222, § 1, dispenses the superior from the necessity of issuing admonitions before punishing the delict. *Per se* the law does not dispense the superior from the necessity of observing the ordinary judicial form. The canon rather concerns the punishment of notorious or specially grave crimes. Notoriety excuses from or dispenses with the necessity of proving those things which are clearly notorious but it does not excuse the superior from the judicial order in which what is notorious is held as proved. [39]

---

37 *"Licet lex nullam sanctionem appositam habeat, tamen Superior potest illius transgressionem, etiam sine praevia poenae comminatione, aliqua iusta poena punire, si scandalum forte datum aut specialis transgressionis gravitas id ferat; secus reus puniri nequit, nisi prius monitus fuerit cum comminatione poenae latae vel ferendae sententiae in casu transgressionis, et nihilominus legem violaverit."*

38 Noval, "De ratione corrigendi," *JP*, III (1923), 39.

39 Regatillo agrees that the delict considered in canon 2222, § 1, constitutes the object of a trial which he outlines according to one of the following forms: (a) the ordinary directs the judge to define both the transgression and the proper punishment; (b) the judge determines the gravity and a proportionate penalty; (c) the ordinary designates the penalty and commands the judge to impose it. *Institutiones Iuris Canonici* (2 vols., Santander: Sal Terrae, 1941-1942. II, 268. Cf. also Muñiz, *Procedimientos*, III, 544.

CHAPTER IV

THE FORM OF THE EXTRAJUDICIAL PROCEDURE BY WAY OF PRECEPT

ARTICLE 1. The General Aspects of this Form

The wide sense of the term *per modum praecepti* is applicable to several processes treated in the Code of Canon Law. It may include those processes administrative in form but which partake at least generally of the nature of a penalty. Thus, canon 2143, § 1, a general norm for the administrative process outlined in the canons following, requires that admonitions be given before witnesses or in writing. As was previously mentioned, this is an admonition to which a precept is attached. [1]

More properly the expression *per modum praecepti* applies to the extrajudicial punishment of crime which is the proper subject of this study. Noval classified these extrajudicial punishments as five in number: [2] (1) the *processus comminatorius,* that is, the giving of a preventive precept to the end that a delinquent may refrain from a repetition of his delict or that one skirting the danger of sin be persuaded to amend his ways; (2) the *processus executorius* under canons 2221, §§ 1 and 4 and 2222, §§ 1 and 2. This is either medicinal or vindicative: medicinal, if the reason for its issuance is the special gravity of the transgression; vindicative, when the cause is some notable scandal; (3) the summary processes of canons 2168-2184; (4) suspension *ex informata conscientia;* (5) the *processus declaratorius,* the declaration of latae sententiae penalties inflicted after the manner of precept. [3]

The *processus comminatorius* consists of two main parts: the *pars praeparatoria* and the *pars constitutiva.* [4] By

---

1 Lega-Bartoccetti, *Commentarius,* III, 174; 194, note 1. Cf. also canons 2168, 2176, 2177, 2182.

2 "De ratione corrigendi" *JP,* III (1923), 205.

3 Canon 2225. Concerning this process, Noval stated that it ought to be used to declare the violation, of itself occult, of the suspension *ex informata conscientia,* if the superior wish to enforce it in the external forum. - "De ratione corrigendi", *JP,* III (1923), 205.

4 Cf. Rainer, *Suspension,* p. 163.

way of preparation, the ordinary must first have recourse to one or several of the penal remedies mentioned in canon 2306, namely admonition, reproof, precept and vigilance. Canon 2307 instructs the ordinary personally or through another to admonish one who is in proximate occasion of committing a delict or who, after investigation, is suspected of having committed a delict. The following canon governs the use of a reproof for one whose manner of acting has given rise to scandal or grave disturbance of the public order. This too may be administered by the ordinary personally or through another or even by letter. Both admonition and reproof may be either public or secret. [5] The former is given before a notary or two witnesses or by letter in such manner that its contents and receipt may appear from some other source. [6] Even though admonition or reproof be secretly administered, proof of its issuance must appear from some other document which must be retained in the secret archives of the curia. [7] These penal remedies may be repeated as often as the ordinary wishes. [8] The natural progression of the various penal remedies and their use do not intrinsically pertain to the manner of proceeding by way of precept. [9]

The nature of the lesser penal remedies, however, is that they pave the way for precept. They can also be used as penal remedies imposed by way of precept, especially since admonition and correction can be made publicly according to canon 2309, § 1. Hence it may be inferred that admonition and reproof comprise a useful but not necessary part of the process by way of precept, since it ought to be established by some document that they were used. [10] Ordinarily admonitions and reproofs should be used since they are well conformed to the spiritual good of the person. Furthermore, as ordained to discover fact and intent, they serve to show moral imputability in their violation. [11] It may be, too, that when a suspect is warned the early stirrings of scandal are removed. Nevertheless, if the faithful

5 Canon 2309, § 1.

6 Canon 2309, § 2.

7 Canon 2309, § 5.

8 Canon 2309, § 6.

9 Lega-Bartoccetti, *Commentarius*, III, 174; Vermeersch-Creusen, *Epitome*, III, 131.

10 Canon 2309, § 5. Cf. also Lega-Bartoccetti, *Commentarius*, III, 192.

11 Lega-Bartoccetti, *Commentarius*, III, 190-191.

believe that there remain certain remote causes or occasions for further evil, the arguments or example of former evil living are not destroyed even though the immediate cause of suspicion be removed. On the other hand, reputation is fully restored if the cause of not only present but also former suspicion be removed.

The various forms of admonition are given by Lega-Bartoccetti: [12] (a) paternal, of which no records are kept; (b) canonical, either secret or public of which a record is preserved in the archives; (c) reprimand and caution prior to the infliction of a censure reprehending and warning a culprit to recede from his contumacy. [13] If a preventive precept contain a threat of censure, the precept itself is sufficient admonition. If a precept threatened a *latae sententiae* penalty, the admonition is likewise included in the precept. Finally, (d) there is the admonition which is itself a penal remedy.

If these milder remedies be ineffectual, or if their impostion be foreseen to be useless, [14] the superior may impose a precept which together with a threat of penalty for its transgression accurately shows what the subject must do or avoid. [15] If the case be grave enough or the subject be in danger of falling into the same crime, the ordinary may also commit the delinquent to be kept under vigilance. This is prescribed especially for recidivists. [16] The decree inflicting vigilance should define when, where, how and before whom the precept should be fulfilled. [17] Correction may be inflicted in place of a penalty [18] and both vigilance and correction may be used to augment a penalty especially for recidivists. [19]

These provisions serve to make more intelligible the law of canon 1933, § 4 which states that penal remedies

---

12 *Commentarius*, III, 192-193.

13 This is proximate to a precept since it contains athreat. Cf. Canons 2233, § 2, and 2242.

14 This often depends on the psychological disposition of the delinquent, for example, his obstinacy, hot temper or on the nature of the crime itself and whether the scandal or neglect is great, widespread or not. - Augustine, *Commentary on the New Code of Canon Law* (8 vols., Vol. VIII, St. Louis: Herder, 1922), VIII, 269.

15 Canon 2310.

16 Canon 2311, § 1.

17 Noval, "De ratione corrigendi", *JP*, III (1923), 36.

18 Canon 2309, § 4.

19 Canons 2309, § 4, and 2311, § 2.

among other penalties can be inflicted by way of precept. Thus it implies that precept, itself a penal remedy, can be inflicted by way of precept. This would be the infliction of a repressive precept (as a penalty for past delicts in transgression of a preventive precept) together with another precept preventive of future delicts. Perhaps an example would serve to illustrate and simplify. From credible witnesses, the ordinary has learned that Father X has repeatedly given scandal by his conduct which has led to at least a suspición of sinful acts or even to actual proof thereof. The ordinary cites Father X to appear before him. Having judged that because of Father X's traits of character an admonition or even a reproof would be ineffectual, the ordinary issues a precept commanding him to avoid frequenting a certain place where it is reasonably believed the evil has occurred. The penalty for disobedience will be suspension. Later it is incontrovertably learned that Father X has broken the precept. Having been again summoned and given a chance to offer an explanation, he is suspended by the ordinary who issues the sentence by way of precept. At the same time, in order to forestall a relapse and to make the occasion of sin still more remote, the ordinary commands Father X not only not to visit the place but also to relinquish his friendship with the inhabitant of that place, and entirely to forego meeting that person under threat of further and still more rigorous penalty.

The case illustrates not only the infliction of penal remedies by way of precept but implicitly shows both the *pars praeparatoria* and the *pars constitutiva.*

Of itself, a sinful act does not constitute a delict for the latter is an external and morally imputable violation of either a law or precept to which there is attached at least an indeterminate canonical sanction. [20] Not every sin is punishable by means of a canonical process or penalty but only that determined by law or precept. "Ordinarily there is no penalty without a law. When a sanction is lacking in the law, at least a precept or admonition must precede before the evil-doer may be chastised." [21]

The imposition of a preventive precept, e g., *de non conversando, de non frequentando,* plainly requires a previous

20 Canon 2195, §§ 1 and 2.

21 Chelodi-Ciprotti, *De Delictis et Poenis,* p. 30; Noval, "De ratione corrigendi", *JP,* III (1923), 49.

cognizance of the fact or rather a full though extrajudicially determined proof [22] of the delict committed or liable to be committed especially in those cases in which prior admonition or reproof was not given. Since admonition and reproof may be omitted, precept is by its very nature a graver remedy. It presupposes guilty conduct deserving punishment. At the same time it offers a last opportunity for amendment. [23] A penal precept has the force or effect similar to that of a condemnatory sentence with suspensive effect. [24] Therefore a preventive precept is both remedial and punitive [25] and this latter element serves to label it grave and liable to cast a heavy shadow over an individual's reputation even though, as was previously stated, the use of a penal remedy may serve to restore good order and incidentally to reestablish trust and confidence. A precept imposed unjustly, either as to mode or matter, gravely impinges on the natural right to good name and repute. Used too easily, too precipitously, without judicious and discreet attempts to ascertain the facts of the case, precept tends to arbitrariness and domination, a far cry from the mildness, order and restraint of canonical procedure and discipline.

The dispensation from the protracted judicial formalities intrinsic to the summary and extrajudicial process of rendering penalties by way of precept does not and cannot dispense from the observance of the elementary principles of justice. Sufficient proof of the violation of the precept must be obtained, the accused must be conceded the opportunity of defending himself and proffering his pleas against the charge of either the delict itself or even the mere suspicion thereof together with commensurate proof to substantiate his claims. [26] Sufficient time must be allowed the accused to enter these pleas or to submit his reasons for his action and to correct his manner of acting. If he neither enters a plea of excuse nor corrects his ways, he

---

22 Romani, *Summa Juris Canonici Lineamenta* (Romae: Apud Auctorem, 1939), p. 268 (Hereafter cited *Summa).*

23 Morsdorf, *Rechtsprechung,* p. 158.

24 Chelodi-Ciprotti, *De Delictis et Poenis,* p. 73; Lega-Bartoccetti, *Commentarius,* III, 174; Roberti, *De Delictis et Poenis,* Vol. I, pars 2, p. 288; Sole, *De Delictis et Poenis,* p. 214; Muñiz, *Procedimientos,* III, 555; Cocchi, *Commentarium,* VIII, 205.

25 According to Morsdorf, a precept cannot itself be a punishment in the strict sense.—*Rechtsprechung,* p. 157.

26 Lega-Bartoccetti, *Commentarius,* III, 191.

is thereby understood to admit the charges. [27] For his part the superior must consider all the circunmstances of law and of fact before he determines and affixes a penalty.

The act of imposing a penalty by way of precept is encompassed by the *pars constitutiva* of this process. When a preventive precept has been transgressed, the superior should proceed to make effective the threat contained in the precept. The superior must first gather information on the transgression so that it stands judicially certain or provable. [28] Unless the delict be notorious, the very nature of the case demands that the investigation or inquisition be made extrajudicially. [29]

The accused must be given the opportunity to enter his plea of explanation or extenuation. If despite protestations of innocence the culpability of the accused is grave, the threatened penalty is inflicted or declared. This infliction, according to canon 2225, should ordinarily be effected in writing or before two witnesses according to the proper form of precept as treated in Chapter II. Unless the public good demand otherwise, the decree may be published in order to enforce its effects publicly. [30]

ARTICLE 2: The Various Opinions concerning Procedure by way of Precept.

Section 1. First Opinion

The cursory and indistinct treatment of penal procept in the Code of Canon Law has given rise to four opinions. In various ways the authors seek to establish the connection between canons 1933, § 4 and 2225. [31]

According to the first opinion, only those penalties listed in canon 1933, § 4 may be inflicted as long as they have been constitued by a particular precept. Thus a precept *ad instar sententiae* can be inflicted to punish the

---

27 Ibid, p. 194.

28 Noval, "De ratione corrigendi", *JP,* III (1923), 36.

29 Wernz-Vidal, *Ius Canonicum,* VII, 204; Roberti, *De Delictis et Poenis,* Vo. I, pars 2, pp. 299-300.

30 Wernz-Vidal, *loc. cit.*

31 These four opinions are summarized and classified by Roberti, *De Delictis et Poenis,* Vol. I, pars 2, p. 293 ff.; "Quaenam poenae";—*Apollinaris,* IV (1931), 294 ff. These are not perfect divisions since some authors differ only slightly with others.

transgression of a precept *ad instar legis.* The penalties enumerated in the canon form an exhaustive list and this canon is modified by canon 2225. Though not holding this opinion, Roberti terms it the strictest interpretation and that which best corresponds to the norms of penal law. [32]

It is clear that the transgression of a precept can be punished extrajudicially by way of a precept. The disagreements among canonists deal with whether the extrajudicial infliction of punishment *per modum praecepti particularis* is solely and exclusively restricted to the trangression of a particular precept and whether other penalties besides those of canon 1933, § 4 may also be so inflicted. Noval is the chief interpreter and proponent of the first opinion. It seems that he is the one who has best explored to date the whole question of this extrajudicial process. His doctrine is briefly explained in his commentary on Part I of the IV Book of the Code, [33] and at greater length but still concisely in the *Jus Pontificium* for 1921-1923. Other who adhere to Noval's opinion are Lega-Bartocetti, [34] Chelodi-Ciprotti, [35] Michiels, [36] Sole, [37] Esswein, [38] Clancy, [39] O'Brien, [40] O'Donnell, [41] Casey. [42]

The purpose of the legislator and the context of the law are the foundation of Noval's opinion. Canon 1933, § 1 states that the delicts which fall under criminal trials are public delicts. The legislator "does not add as *prima facie* it seems he ought to have added that the delicts which can

---

32 *Loc. cit.;* cf. also Coronata, *Institutiones,* III, 378.

33 *De Iudiciis,* p. 173

34 *Commentarius,* III, 197.

35 *De Delictis et Poenis,* p. 166.

36 "De reservationae censurae *latae sententia praecepto peculiari adnexae". Ephemerides Theologicae Lovaniensis,* IV (1927), 181; 191. Although Roberti presents Michiels as maintaining the third opinion, his doctrine seems consonant with Noval's.

37 *De Delictis et Poenis,* n. 102-103.

38 *The Extrajudicial Coercive Powers of Ecclesiastical Superiors,* The Catholic University of America Canon Law Studies, No. 127. (Washington, D. C.: The Catholic University of America Press, 1941), p. 110 ff.

39 *The Local Religious Superior,* The Catholic University of America Canon Law Studies, No. 175. (Washington, D. C.: The Catholic University of America Press, 1943), p. 110 ff.

40 *The Provincial Religious Superior,* The Catholic University of America Canon Law Studies, No. 258, (Washington, D. C.: The Catholic University of America Press, 1947), pp. 238, 246, 253.

41 *The Marriage of Minors,* The Catholic University of America Canon Law Studies, No. 221. (Washington, D. C.: The Catholic University of America Press, 1945), p. 188 ff.

42 *A Study of Canon 2222, § 1,* pp. 89, 93, 94.

be punished extrajudicially are occult delicts... but delicts which can be punished by way of precept. These... are only those which consist in the violation of a particular precept. Regularly and of themselves they are occult". [43] In case of transgression another precept is required to inflict the threatened penalty. In the case of a *latae sententiae* penalty, however, the second precept is unnecessary. [44] But the precept may be used, however, for the declaration of the penalty.

Canon 2225 dealing with the form of precept taken together with canon 2310 on preventive precept and canon 1933, § 4 on precept as a mode of procedure proves that the transgression of precept can ordinarily be punished by the summary process. [45] Canon 2225 supposes and canon 1933, § 4 expresses the fact that some delicts can be punished extrajudicially. Furthermore, canon 2225 adds that these delicts can regularly be punished extrajudicially. [46] This canon, in Noval's estimation, definitely and exclusively indicates the form of penal precept. [47]

According to this first opinion, the phrase *inflicta sit* of canon 2225 means *statuta sit* and *ordinarie* is interpreted strictly in respect to the observance of the form of precept.

While strict in interpretation of the canons dealing with the subject of precept, this opinion thereby deals benignly with the culprit through its restriction of the extrajudicial process in which there is greater chance of arbitrariness on the part of the superior. A penal precept cannot be inflicted unless in each case its reasonable basis is sufficiently clear, namely, the cause of the penalty (the delict), its perpetrator, his imputability, the proper proportion between the crime and the penalty, and the hope of

---

43 Noval, "De ratione corrigendi", *JP*, II (1922), 155.

44 Coronata, *Institutiones*, III, 379; *AAS*, XII (1920), 357; Bouscaren, *The Canon Law Digest* (2 vols., Milwaukee: Bruce, 1934-1943), I, 845. (Hereafter cited *The Canon Law Digest*).

45 S. R. Rota, Pharen *"Iurium et Poenanum"*, 10 iun 1910 coram R. P. Guilelmo Sebastianelli, Dec. XX, n. 7 - *S.R.R. Decis, II* (1910), 195.

46 Noval, "De ratione corrigendi", *JP*, III (1923), 36.

47 The positions of these canons in the Code of Canon Law are indications of incomplete and inexact legislation. Canon 2225 expresses the legitimate modes of inflicting penalties and pertaining to procedure more properly belongs in the Fourth Book. On the other hand, canon 1933, § 4 pertains to penal law and hence belongs in Book Five. Cf. Roberti, *De Delictis et Poenis*, 293; Morsdorf, *Rechtsprechung*, p. 159; Cappello, *De Censuris* (ed. altera. Taurinorum Augustae; Marietti, 1925), p. 76.

accomplishing the goal of the judgment.[84] The benign interpretation is according to the spirit of the Code. Inasmuch as the whole question deals with the infliction of penalties, this opinion which is mild should be followed. The Code lacks any prescription which would call for a more severe interpretation. The enumeration of penalties in canon 1933, § 4 would be useless if all other penalties could be inflicted by way of precept.[49]

The objections to this explanation are: (1) that it is the practice of the curias both Roman and local to follow the less strict opinions since they offer a practical manner of dealing with delinquents; (2) that Noval's interpretation is too involved when is question of minor penalties; (3) that the necessity for providing for the common good demands a more facile application of penalties than that envisioned by Noval; (4) that the understanding of *inflicta sit* as *statuta sit* is a grave distortion of the text;[50] and (5) that confining the imposition of penalty by way of precept would give an already convicted lawbreaker a time of grace to which he has no right and in which he might effect something harmful to the community.[51]

To the first objection, Coronata[52] sagely remarks that whether the practice is legitimate or an abuse must first be determined. The correct practice is indicated in canon 1933, § 4 or by other canons which provide special procedures. Since the Code of Canon Law has abrogated all universal pre-Code penal customs they can subsequently be reintroduced only with great difficulty.[53]

To the appeal to the necessity of providing for the common good, the same author, basing his opinion on canons 20 and 2219, rightly rejoins that especially in view of the fact that any extensive interpretation of penal law must be avoided, this objection argues rather for an enactment of a new law than the extension of an already existing

---

48 Noval, "De ratione corrigendi", *JP*, III (1923), 204.

49 Coronata, *Institutiones*, III, 378; Chelodi-Ciprotti, *De Delictis ta Poenis*, p. 166; Wernz-Vidal, *Ius Canonicum*, VII, 204.

50 Bouscaren-Ellis, *Canon Law, a Text and Commentary* (Milwaukee: Bruce, 1946), p. 805 (cited hereafter as *Canon Law*). These authors, however, assert that this does violence not to the text but to the radical meaning of the verb and attributes to canon 2225 an effect which is entirely foreign to its setting and context, namely, the modification of canon 1933, § 4.

51 Morsdorf, *Rechtsprechung*, p. 160.

52 *Institutiones*, III, 378.

53 Cf. Roberti, *De Delictis et Poenis*, Vol. I, pars 1, pp. 81-82.

law. Chelodi-Ciprotti [54] add that the necessity of providing for the good of souls is already taken care of by other canons which allow the infliction of penalties or the application of remedies without observance of the judicial order. [55]

Section 2. Second Opinion

According to the second opinion, all the penalties mentioned in canon 1933, § 4 can be inflicted or declared by way of precept whether they were constituted by law or precept. All other penalties can be inflicted only by judicial process. *Inflicta sit* in canon 2225 is taken as *infligatur.* This interpretation also does some violence to the verb, but, according to Bouscaren-Ellis [56] the distortion is less than that wrought by the first opinion which insists on the past tense of the verb as meaning *statuta sit.*

The chief proponents of this interpretation are Cappello. [57] Bouscaren-Ellis [58] and Morsdorf. [59]

This exposition labors under the obvious difficulty of grave inequalty since it allows grave penalties to be inflicted by way of precept but requires a judicial process for lighter penalties which are not mentioned in canon 1933, § 4. In practice, however, light penalties are actually inflicted by way of precept. [60] In justification of his support of the theory, Morsdorf [61] lays the fault for what he calls the mistake made by the proponents of the first theory on the deficient composition of canon 2225 and the passive form of *inflicta sit.* According to Morsdorf, the parallel between canons 2225 and 1933, § 4 clearly establishes only the different forms of procedure and is not concerned with

---

54 *De Delictis et Poenis,* p. 166; Cf. also Blat, *Commentarium* p. 477. Bouscaren, *The Canon Law Digest,* I, 622; *AAS,* IX (1917), 328.

55 E. g., canons 188; 454, § 4; 471, § 3; 595, § 3; 646; 654; 970; 2222, §§ 1 and 2; 1340.

56 *Canon Law,* p. 805.

57 *De Censuris,* n. 76. Cappello's indefinite statements *(De Censuris,* ed altera. No. 14 and 76; *Periodica* XIX (1930) pp. 36-38) regarding the function of canon 2225 may have been the cause of Roberti's ascribing him as holding the second, third and fourth opinions *(De Delictis et Poenis,* Vol I, pars 2, p. 293 ff.; "Quaenam poenae" - *Apollinaris* IV (1931), pp. 296-298). However, since the article in *Periodica* was published several years after the second edition of *De Censuris,* it probably conveys his real opinion.

58 *Loc. cit.*

59 Rechtsprechung, p. 160.

60 Roberti, *De Delictis et Poenis,* Vol. I, pars 2. p. 295.

61 *Op cit.,* pp. 160-163.

the suppositions or causes for any particular procedure.[62] Thus, the extrajudicial infliction of punishment is similar to a sentence and like a sentence can be applied after any threat of penalty promulgated by law or precept. According to this opinion, the enumeration of penalties in canon 1933, § 4 is an exhaustive or exclusive list. Considered otherwise, it would impose an intolerable yoke.

Section 3. Third Opinion

The third opinion claims that not only the penalties mentioned in canon 1933, § 4 and which have been enacted by law but also any other penalty whatsoever when constituted by precept can be inflicted by way of precept. Proponents of this opinion are Chelodi,[63] Vermeersch-Creusen,[64] Cappello[65] and Muñiz.[66]

Canon 2225, according to this theory, completes canon 1933, § 4. Ordinarily penalties constituted by precept may be inflicted or declared by way of precept. Canon 2225, therefore, is read as if it stated "if a penalty is constituted by precept and inflicted by way of precept." This theory finds its justification for its interpretation of "inflicted" as "constituted" in canon 2220, § 2 which denes to the vicar general the power of inflicting (or constituting) penalties.

This interpretation is forced to find justification for precept itself since if every penalty of law can be inflicted extrajudicially, the preventive precept is a weak and almost useless institute. The ordinary criminal procedure is also useless for the most part. The practical necessity of efficaciously dealing with particular cases in which precepts have been imposed is the justification advanced for this interpretation. The cases are usually well known and hardly need a long judicial inquisition. Similarly minor penalties or disciplinary action for offenses against one's office or duty and those which admit of the administrative process can be constituted and applied by way of precept.

The practice of the curias well corresponds to this

---

62 Cf. also Bouscaren-Ellis, *Canon Law*, p. 805.

63 *Ius Poenale* (3 ed., Tridenti, 1933), p. 27.

64 *Epitome*, III, 415.

65 *De Censuris* (ed. altera), nn. 14 and 76.

66 *Procedimientos, III*, 47.

opinion.[67] Vermeersch-Creusen[68] state that for the transgression of a precept the ordinary ought not to have recourse to a trial in order to declare or inflict a penalty. The proponents of the first opinion, on the contrary, would always permit a formal trial in a case of the public infraction of a preventive precept.

The formalities for the infliction of penalties according to this mode are exceedingly brief. Having certain knowledge of the violation of a precept, and having heard the accused, the superior can inflict the penalty which he himself has constituted. Even if it appear certain that a delict were already committed in violation of a law or even without a prior precept, a penalty can be inflicted or declared.[69]

Section 4. Fourth Opinion

The fourth opinion was proposed by Cappello,[70] Roberti,[71] Wernz-Vidal,[72] Berutti,[73] and Regatillo.[74]

The viewpoint of these authors is that there is no exclusive clause in canon 1933, § 4 and that canon 2225 indiscriminately allows use of either judicial or extrajudicial procedure. Consequently, these canonists construe *infligere* as meaning *applicare* especially when used in connection with the extrajudicial process. They too consider the past tense of *inflicta sit* as a misuse. The present *infligatur* would have been more exact and proper.

Canon 1933, § 4 does not furnish an exhaustive list of penalties which may be applied by way of penal precept. Cappello contends that if excommunication, the gravest of penalties, can be inflicted by way of precept, so can any other penalty.[75] Indeed, it is remarkable that while the judicial sentence of excommunication must be passed by a

---

67 Roberti, *De Delictis et Poenis*, Vol. I, pars 2, p. 295.

68 *Epitome*, III, 132; 247.

69 Cappello, *Summa Iuris Canonici* (3 vols., Vol. III, Romae: Apud Aedes Universitatis Gregorianae, 1936), III, 309. (Hereafter cited as *Summa*).

70 "Irrogatio poenae per modum praecepti extraiudicium" - *Periodica*, XIX (1930), 36. (Cited hereafter as "Irrogatio poenae" - *Periodica*).

71 *De Delictis et Poenis*, Vol. I, pars 2, p. 296; "Quaenam poenae" - *Apollinaris*, IV (1931), 294-300.

72 *Ius Canonicum*, VII, 205-206.

73 *Institutiones*, VI, 83.

74 *Institutiones*, II, 353.

75 *Summa*, III, 309; Vermeersch-Creusen, III, 131.

tribunal of three judges,[76] the extrajudicial mode based on only a summary knowledge and procedure depends on the judgment of the superior alone.[77] The interpretation followed by these canonists is that any penalty constituted by law or precept, with the exception of those for which special processes are required can be inflicted extrajudicially. The extrinsic arguments adduced to support this exposition are: (1) the punishment of occult crimes is properly provided for, including occult delicts in transgression of precepts. Thus occult delicts would be punishable not only by suspension *ex informata conscientia*[78] or by administrative provisions of canon 2147, § 2, n. 4[79] but also by way of penal precept; (2) the practice of the curias and Roman Congregations follows this interpretation. Not infrequently these authorities apply penalties by way of precept even for delicts defined in the common law. This argument appeals to canon 20 which covers those cases in which there is lacking any prescript of law and which provides the practice of the Roman Curias as one of the norms to be followed. The proponents of the fourth opinion seem to have overlooked the clause contained within that canon which clause, *"nisi agatur de poenis applicandis"*, nullifies the appeal to this norm.

Furthermore, it may be objected that the limits of the extrajudicial procedure are indefinite and that the natural order certainly requires a proper procedure for the application of penalties. This opinion, however, considers this tenet of the natural law as only relative and not absolute. Positive law, especially where minor offenses are concerned, can dispense from this provision. Likewise, the necessity of providing for the common good bestows a dispensation or mitigation of this natural right. But the common law nowhere expresses such a dispensation or mitigation and while this interpretation may seem to be a mild and benign one, it is so only to the extent of freeing the superior from definite restrictions of law. As far as the culprit to whom the penalties are applied is concerned, this interpretation appears rather harsh and odious.

---

76 Canon 1576, § 1, n. 1.

77 Wernz-Vidal, *Ius Canonicum*, VII, 204.

78 Canon 2186.

79 An irremovable pastor can be removed for a *"probabile crimen occlutum, parocho imputatum, ex quo Ordinarius prudenter praevidet magnam in posterum oriri posse fidelium offensionem."*

Although canon 2193, § 3, n. 3 dispenses from the formality of a trial when it may be impossible, useless or harmful to conduct one, it does not seem to provide a parallel norm for determining the scope of the extrajudicial process by way of precept. Suspension *ex informata conscientia* is a most extraordinary procedure to cover rare cases. The analogy, therefore, is uncertain and doubtful. [80]

ARTICLE 3. The Concept of the Word of "Certain" in Canon 1933, § 4.

Canon 1933, § 4 rigidly restricts the operation of the extrajudicial process to those cases in which the delict is certain. This is an attempt to prevent the arbitrary application of punishments without judicial formalities, [81] and to safeguard the rights of the individual even while providing the ecclesiastical superiors with an effective means for the prompt and summary treatment of crime and the protection of the common good.

Though procedure by way of precept may be termed an informal process in contradistinction to the judicial or formal procedure, the extrajudicial process retains the basic measures to preserve justice and prevent that harsh and unnatural prostitution of justice which condemns without reason or mercy. The superior may dispense with the use of admonitions or reproofs or both in individual cases in accord with the faculty contained in canon 2310. Yet, in such an event, he may thereby ignore one of the most useful means to discover the deed and intent of the culprit as well as his moral imputability. It may be that in an individual case justice may also be slighted in consequence of the omission of preliminary warnings since the person is deprived of the occasion to proffer his pleas concerning the suspicion of his guilt or even against the delict itself. [82]

---

80 The following is illustrative both of the analogy wrought here and of the restriction of the rights of the individual. "Where a process be impossible, entirely useless or even harmful to the good of souls by reason of scandal or damage derived therefrom, or by reason of particular circumstances of person or place, a penalty can be inflicted on a delinquent by way of precept, as often as the delict be certain. Justice itself demands this, for otherwise, if a trial were impossible, justice would not be served at all. The nature and the complexity of the judicial order advocate this practice... since trials should be avoided as much as possible." - Cappello, "Irrogatio poenae",- *Periodica*, XIX (1930), 36-38.

81 Morsdorf, *Rechtsprechung*, p. 162; Lega-Bartoccetti, *Commentarius*, III, 189.

82 Lega-Bartoccetti, *Commentarius*, III, 191.

A custom of by-passing admonition and reproof in favor of precept would constitute a mode of action in violation of the Code, a practical denial of the rights of the individual, an arbitrary and capricious domination far removed from the well-ordered regimen of ecclesiastical discipline, a spirit contradicting canon 2214, § 2, and the Council of Trent. [83]

The concept of the word "certain" may be derived from several parallell passages in the Code. Canon 2233, § 1, states that no penalty can be inflicted unless it appears with certainty that a delict was committed and legal prescription has not accrued. Regarding the determination of the act in the transgression of the precept as constituting a real delict, Morsdorff [84] considers canon 1869 on the construction of certainty as applicable. This canon requires the judge to act with moral certitude derived from the acts and proofs. I tis the judge's own conscience which estimates the weight of these proofs. Should he be unable to form such certitude, the judge must dismiss the accused. Outside the formalities of a judicial trial, it is often difficult if not impossible to sift the manifold evidences and proofs offered in either condemnation or extenuation. [85]

If in a particular case, it would be impossible to determine guilt without a judicial trial, the summary procedure could be not used. This is a safe guarantee that an innocent person will not be unjustly condemned. At the same time, one must remember that the formalities of strict judicial proof cannot be demanded to the same degree in an extrajudicial procedure. The norm is taken from the formal procedure and applied to the informal. [86] The judgment on the deed itself must consider all its subjective and objective qualities for the penal canons which consider these factors are as applicable to violation of precept as to violation of law. [87] Hence the need of an investigation to determine the transgression of the precept itself as to both fact and imputability derived from malice unmitigated by any excusing cause. This certitude demanded in canon 1933, § 4 is more rigorous than that demanded in canons 2307 and

83 Sess. XIII, c. 1.

84 *Rechtsprechung*, p. 162.

85 *Ibid.*

86 Blat, *De Delictis et Poenis*, p. 452.

87 Canon 2228.

following for there even danger of sin or grave suspicion of one's having committed a delict is sufficient ground for imposing a preventive precept.[88] To hold an investigation is the rule; to dispense with it should be the exception.[89]

If the transgression be notorious, there is usually no necessity of hearing to determine the fact since it is proved by its very notoriety.[90] Nevertheless the accused should receive an opportunity to present a legitimate defense and to demonstrate his innocence. If, however, an imputed delict is not denied, or if it is evident or notorious, a hearing may be neither useful nor necessary. So, too, if after a judicial sentence has been imposed the convicted person raises unfounded exceptions to delay his observance of the sentence, the ordinary could impose a precept to enforce compliance. If the precept is not obeyed, the penal sanction threatened in the precept may then be inflicted.[91]

Canon 1933, § 1 restricts the judicial trial to public delicts. The interpretation of paragraph four offered by Noval and adopted here does not find an opposition between these paragraphs as meaning public delicts and occult delicts respectively but as meaning public delicts and delicts committed in violation of a precept. Ordinarily these latter transgressions will be occult at least formally since the imposition of a precept is secret as far as the general body of the faithful is concerned. This preserves the general rule of paragraph one since law is ordained to govern what happens ordinarily and normally and not what happens rarely as, for example, the public violations of precept.[92]

Sipos[93] and Romani[94] restrict the extrajudicial procedure to occult delicts which restriction is indeed true for the suspension *ex informata conscientia* but implicity overlooks the whole concept of procedure by way of precept.

---

88 Noval, "De ratione corrigendi", *JP*, II (1922), 156.

89 Morsdorf, *Rechtsprechung*, p. 166; Roberti, *De Delictis et Poenis*, Vol. I, pars 2, pp. 299-300.

90 Morsdorf, *loc. cit.;* Roberti, *loc. cit.;* Wernz-Vidal, *Ius Canonicum*, VII, 204.

91 Lega-Bartoccetti, *Commentarius*, III, 189.

92 Noval, "De ratione corrigendi...", *JP* 1 (1922), 156.

93 *Enchiridion*, p. 869.

94 *Summa*, p. 220.

The essential point is the actual transgression of the precept whether the delict be public or occult. [95]

The notion of certainty is more restricted and less comprehensive than that of probability. Before punishing by way of precept, the superior must be morally certain of the delict and its imputability. This is a *condicio sine qua non.* [96] Usually moral certitude is reached by judicial discussion and when this is by-passed, certitude must be obtained from other sources. In the preparatory stages of the entire process by precept, probability or suspicion or even the danger of sin offers sufficient grounds for imposing a preventive precept. [97]

Canon 1933, § 4 concerns the imposition of a repressive precept for the certain violation of the preventive precept. The investigation should seek clearly and precisely and directly to discover the transgression of the precept itself and not primarily the actual or suspected violation of the law which was the cause for the precept.

---

95 Noval, *loc. cit.; Cappello,* Summa, III, 309: "Irrogatio poenae...", *Periodica,* XIX 1930), 36; Vermeersch-Creusen, *Epitome,* III, 132.

96 Cappello, *loc. cit.*

97 Canon 2307.

CHAPTER V

THE PENALTIES WHICH MAY BE INFLICTED EXTRA-JUDICIALLY BY WAY OF PRECEPT

ARTICLE 1. The Penalties of the Extrajudicial Procedure.

Section 1. General Norms.

The scope of penalties encompassed by canon 1933, § 4 is extraordinarily wide including not only the mild canonical penances and remedies but also the stringent and drastic chastisements of suspension, interdict and excommunication.

It is evidently in keeping with their nature that penances and penal remedies can be inflicted extrajudicially since they are primarily medicinal and tend to forestall the burden, difficulty and protracted discussion of a trial through their opportune use.[1] In fact, the entire canon is primarily but not exclusively medicinal. It is most feasible that clerics or laics whom it would be useless to prosecute in the ecclesiastical judicial forum be confronted with an action more loving and paternal. Should the medicinal remedy be unacceptable to the criminal, it still serves the purpose of helping to prevent scandal.[2]

Admonition, reproof, precept and vigilance are penal remedies in themselves and as such can precede the application of a precept as an act of that process in which they may be inflicted as penalties. It is the nature of penal remedies that they pave the way for procedure by way of precept but they can also be threatened by precept especially since admonition and reproof can become public by virtue of canon 2309, § 5.[3] Admonition and reproof may precede precept or precept may be imposed without the

---

1 Noval, *De Iudiciis*, 495; Cappello, *Summa*, III, 309; Chelodi, *Ius Poenale*, p 114.

2 Lega-Bartoccetti, *Commentarius*, III, 188.

3 *Ibid.*, pp. 174-175, 188, 190.

prior use of either admonition or reproof.[4] The law gives no indication whether vigilance may also precede precept but it is in accord with its nature that it may so precede.

The extrajudicial manner of inflicting penances and penal remedies is sufficiently accomplished according to the provisions of canon 2225. Coronata takes issue with both Chelodi and Noval who seem to exclude the obligation of observing this canon in aplying penances and penal remedies. It seems to Coronata that this formality is required by canon 1933, § 4 which commands that even penalties and penal remedies must be imposed *ad modum praecepti.* "Perhaps it can be said that the form of canon 2225 is obligatory only in case a special form does not exist as in inflicting penances and penalties and not in penal remedies for which the Code prescribes a special form."[5]

There may be occasion for the superior to chose between these extremes in the punishment of the transgression of a precept. The degree of certitude which he possesses would necessarily dictate the particular penalty. Thus, the superior may have only slight indications or incomplete reports of the commission of a delict or of the proximate danger of evil-doing, as for example, the report of only one trustworthy person. In such an event, the ordinary should have recourse only to using secret and paternal remedies, namely paternal admonitions and reproofs.[6] From the imposition of such mild remedies, the accused suffers little external detriment and a great deal of spiritual good may come from them.[7]

On the other hand, should the accused either confess or be legally convicted through arguments which he has unsuccessfully contested, the delinquent may be punished extrajudicially by means of public remedies. Confession and conviction in this case are both extrajudicial, that is, a confession freely and knowingly made or a conviction through incontestable testimony of trustworthy persons who, for a just cause, may not be prepared to give their testimony in a trial. The confession made in this manner,

4 Cf. p. 40 for the classification of admonition as paternal, canonical (that is, public and secret penal remedies), and as a reprimand. Paternal admonition is not a penal remedy.

5 *Institutiones*, III, 379-380, note 1.

6 Noval, *De Iudiciis*, p. 496; "De ratione corrigendi", *JP*, III (1923), 206.

7 Noval, *De Iudiciis*, p. 496.

though sufficient for the imposition of an extrajudicial penal remedy is not conclusive proof for condemnation in a formal trial. [8]

Some authors [9] think that an informal and private precept is valid and sustainable by extrajudicial enforcement. The precept they are considering in this manner is that according to canon 24 and not the preventive precept of canon 2310. Lega-Bartoccetti state that the transgression of an informal precept can be punished in the external forum but if the subject refuse to undergo the penalties, they cannot be judicially enforced since legitimate proof is lacking. An informal precept derived from voluntary extrajudicial jurisdiction retains its force in the external but non-judicial forum to which the subject has a right of recourse. [10]

The extrajudicial criminal procedure extends also to the infliction of censures. If the superior possesses legislative power, he may inflict censures *ad instar legis.* Should the superior possess only jurisdictional and not legislative power, as in the case with local superiors of exempt clerical religious, this non-ordinary may punish by means of censures only by way of a particular precept. [11] The Code itself makes no determination of what types of precepts are included under canon 2220, § 1. But its position within the treatment of penal law argues for those imposed through jurisdictional power and not mere dominative power by which a superior would command a subject *in virtute sanctae obedientiae.* Canons 2307-2309, however, restrict to the ordinary the application of admonitions and reproofs. Canon 2310 in dealing with precept makes no mention of the ordinary but the context evidently presupposes the ordinary as the competent authority. The local religious superior, therefore, cannot impose these canonical penal remedies. However, it would seem warranted to conclude

---

8 Noval, "De ratione corrigendi", *JP,* III (1923), 206.

9 E.g., Coronata, *Institutiones,* IV, 108; Cocchi *Commentarium,* VII, 436; Maroto, *Institutiones,* I, 295; Cicognani, *Canon Law,* p. 638; Lega-Bartocetti, *Commentarius,* III, 195.

10 *Commentarius,* III, 195.

11 Canon 2220, § 1. *Qui pollent potestate leges ferendi vel praecepta imponendi, possunt quoque legi vel praecepto poenas adnectare; qui iudiciali tantum, possunt solummodo poenas, legitime statutas, ad norman iuris applicare.*

that the superior can issue these admonitions, reproofs and precepts in a manner similar to the canonical institutes.[12]

For the infliction of censures, the provisions of canons 2233, §2 and 2242, §§ 2 and 3 should be observed, namely, the administration of admonitions, the granting of sufficient time to reform and repent and a just estimation of contumacy according to the norms of the canons. Of course, the precept itself contains an admonition in the very threat of penalty.

Section 2. The Penalties Proper to the Extrajudicial Procedure by way of Precept.

Canon 1933, § 4 gives no indication whether the penalties (other than excommunication which is always medicinal) are to be considered as either medicinal or vindicative. In the Instruction of 1880 penances were termed penal remedies. The present law unites penances and penal remedies as the third type of ecclesiastical punishments,[13] but treats of penances in a separate chapter.[14] The inclusion of penal remedies and penances within the same title indicates the general intent of the legislator as purposing to procure the emendation of a delinquent, to evoke signs of repentance and to render remote danger of scandal.

The other great penalties mentioned in canon 1933, § 4, interdict and suspension, may be either medicinal or vindicative. It is certain, therefore, that the nature of these penalties is at least medicinal.[15] The authors extend the application of canon 1933, § 4 to vindicative penalties[16] for, if vindicative penalties were excluded from the extrajudicial process, the whole legal institute of penal precept would be rendered less effective.[17] Since they are of a

---

12 Noval, *De Iudiciis*, p. 496 ff.; "De ratione corrigendi", *JP*, II (1922), 206. This question of the power of the religious superior will be examined in Chapter VI.

13 Canon 2216.

14 Canons 2312 ff.

15 Noval, "De ratione corrigendi", *JP*, III (1923), 37; Lega-Bartoccetti, *Commentarius*, III, 190; Morsdorf, *Rechtsprechung*, p. 164; Sipos, *Enchiridion*, p. 869.

16 Lega-Bartoccetti, *op. cit.*, III, 174; Morsdorf, *op. cit.*, p. 165; Berutti, *Institutiones*, VI, 238; Roberti, *De Delictis et Poenis*, Vol. I, pars 2, p. 296; Blat, *De Processibus*, p. 452; Romani, *Summa*, p. 220.

17 If one were punished according to the ruling of canon 2222, § 1, the penalty would be vindicative, from the nature of the canon. Cf. Blat, *De Processibus*, p. 452.

definitely stipulated duration, vindicative penalties are in that manner milder than medicinal,[18] and are in complete harmony with the benignity of the legislator. As regards the understanding of canon 1933, § 4 as medicinal or vindicative, Bouscaren-Ellis adopt the more restricted view that the infliction of vindicative penalties requires the full judicial proof.[19]

Wernz-Vidal[20] call sharp attention to the fact that to declare or inflict an excommunication through judicial sentence in a trial three judges are required for the validity of the proceedings. Nevertheless excommunication, severest of ecclesiastical penalties, can be inflicted extrajudicially by way of precept by the competent superor alone observing only the formalities of canon 2225, which form is not rigorously required.[21]

Some authors claim that interdict and suspension may be inflicted as either censures or vindicative penalties.[22] Others, however, consider that these penalties can be inflicted only as censures.[23] One case which had gone to the Rota on appeal was regarded as an infliction of a penalty by way of precept as both a medicinal and a vindicative punishment.[24]

Section 3. The Penalties Excluded from the Extrajudicial Procedure.

By positive provision the Code of Canon Law establishes special procedures for particular matters either penal or administrative. The authors who hold to an extremely wide interpretation of canon 1933, § 4, make this canon applicable to almost every penal and disciplinary action. Cappello, for example, to justify his contention that any penalty whatsoever can be inflicted extrajudicially,

---

18 Morsdorf, *op. cit.* p. 165.

19 *Canon Law,* p. 805.

20 *Ius Canonicum,* VII, 204-205.

21 Cf. p. 23.

22 Coronata, *Institutiones,* III, 377; Blat, *De Processibus,* p. 477; Cappello, "Irrogatio poenae...", - *Periodica,* XIX (1930), 37; Roberti, "Quaenam poenae...", - *Apollinaris,* IV (1930), 294.

23 Noval, *De Iudiciis,* pp. 755-756; Augustine, *Commentary,* VIII, 358; Wernz-Vidal, *Ius Canonicum,* VI, 703.

24 S. R. Rota, *"Jurium et Poenarum",* 10 Iun. 1910, *coram* R. P. D. *Guilelmo Sebastianelli, Decis.* XI, *S. R. R.* Decis. II (1910), 191.

draws an analogy from the provisions of canon 2191, § 3, n. 3 which dispenses from the observance of the judicial procedure in punishing public delicts by means of a suspension *ex informata conscientia* when witnesses refuse to testify, or when the accused cleric hinders the judicial process, or when civil law or danger of grave scandal impedes the formal procedure. Wernz-Vidal also hold to the wide interpretation. While they admit that the enumeration of penalties in canon 1933, § 4 is complete and exhaustive, they nevertheless extend its application to penalties less grave than those mentioned in the canon.

Since the adherents of the first opinion understand canon 1933, § 4 as applicable only to the transgression of a preventive particular precept, the limits of this canon are already clearly defined by their interpretation and it is unnecessary to appeal to other canons which expressly require the judicial or special administrative process. On the other hand, those canonists who seem to extend the ambit of this canon so as to include penalties other than those mentioned within the canon itself while including other penalties, must attempt to define the limits of the extrajudicial process. [25]

Section 4. The Effects of Penalties Inflicted by way of Precept.

The Code of Canon Law nowhere speaks of the effects of penal precept but confines itself to recounting the effects of a judicial sentence. Roberti [26] states that the practice of the Roman Curia is to consider the effects of a penal pre-

---

25 Wernz-Vidal, *Ius Canonicum*, VII, 205; Regatillo, *Institutiones*, II, 353; Roberti, *De Delicts et Poenis*, Vol. I, pars 2, pp. 292, 296. The canons which demand special penal or administrative processes are: canon 192, § 2, the deprivation of an irremovable incumbent of his office; canon 1576, § 1, 1°, the necessity of a collegiate tribunal in criminal trials for the deprivation of office; canon 1576, § 1, 2°, the collegiate tribunal necessary for any sentence of deposition, perpetual deprivation of ecclesiastical garb or degradation; canon 2303, deposition and its concomitant penalties; canon 2304, the deprivation of ecclesiastical garb; canon 2305, degradation and its allied effects. All these can be inflicted only by means of a judicial sentence. On the other hand, by canon 1555, § 1, the tribunal of the Holy Office follows its own special procedure and inferior courts delegated by this tribunal follow the norms imposed by the superior court. Canons 2142-2194 contain expressly defined procedures for the removal of irremovable pastors, for punishing clerics illegally absent from their benefices, for punishing clerics guilty of concubinage, for punishing pastors negligent in fulfilling their office and the infliction of a suspension *ex informata conscientiae*. The judicial dismissal of religious in exempt clerical orders is outlined in canons 654 and following and the administrative dismissal of non-exempt religious in canons 649 and following.

26 De Delictis et Poenis, Vol. I, pars 2, p. 301.

cept the same as those of a sentence. Cappello[27] declares that if the precept be published either in the *Acta Apostolica Sedis*[28] or in some official diocesan publication, the precept has the same juridical effects as a sentence. Roberti[29] asserts that the decision ought to be conveyed to the guilty cleric and that if the effects are to be enforced publicly, the penalty should be published.

The effects which are applicable to penalties inflicted by way of precept as well as to those inflicted by judicial sentence are contained in the following canons: canon 167, § 3, n. 3, loss of the right of suffrage after a sentence imposing a censure which carries with it infamy of law; canon 765, § 2, prohibition of an excommunicate to act as sponsor at baptism after a condemnatory or a declaratory sentence; canon 795, § 2, the same prohibition to act as sponsor at confirmation under the same circumstances; canon 1095, § 1, n. 1, loss of the right of the pastor to assist at matrimony after a condemnatory or a declaratory sentence of excommunication, suspension or interdict; canon 1240, § 1, n. 2, deprivation of ecclesiastical burial; canon 2260, § 1, loss of right to receive the sacraments after excommunication and the further loss of right to the sacramentals after a condemnatory or a declaratory sentence of excommunication; canon 2261, §§ 1 and 2, prohibition to confect and or administer the sacraments after excommunication except upon a request by the faithful for a just cause or in danger of death; canon 2261, § 3, the right of the faithful to request sacramental absolution from a priest who has been excommunicated by means of a condemnatory or a declaratory sentence or from one who is *vitandus* only in danger of death and, if worthy ministers are unavailable, also the other sacraments and sacramentals;[30] canon 2264, acts of jurisdiction exercised by one who has been suspended by a condemnatory or a declaratory sentence or after revocation of the power of jurisdiction by the superior are invalid as provided in canon 2261, § 3; canon 2266, after a sentence or declaration of excommunication, the person remains deprived of the fruits of his dignity, office, benefice,

27 "Irrogatio poenae...", - *Periodica,* XIX (1930), 36*-38*. Cf. also Chelodi, *Ius Poenale,* p. 25.

28 E.g., *AAS,* XXII (1930), 138.

29 *Loc. cit.*

30 This same provision would apply in the case in which a priest would be excommunicated by way of precept.

pension, position; canon 2275, those under personal interdict cannot celebrate or assist at divine offices and may assist only at sermons and instructions; canon 2248, those who have contracted a suspension which prohibits the administration of the sacraments and sacramentals are bound by the provision of canon 2261.

CHAPTER VI

SUPERIOR AND SUBJECT UNDER THE EXTRA-JUDICIAL PROCEDURE BY WAY OF PRECEPT

ARTICLE 1. The Competent Superior

It is not easy to determine exactly who are the ecclesiastical superors competent to impose a precept and to inflict a penalty for its non-observance. The law as contained in canon 2220, § 1 merely states that they who enjoy the power of passing laws or of imposing precepts can also attach penalties to the law or precept. But this gives no direct indication of the proper authorities for imposing a precept. It is clear, of course, that inasmuch as penal precept is treated in Books IV and V of the Code, which postulate actual and full ecclesiastical jurisdiction, those superiors who exercise jurisdiction in the external forum are constituted lawful officials for administering penal precepts.

There will be little debate or discussion regarding the power of those officials or assemblies which are expressly given legislative authority and which are endowed with the power of imposing penalties.

It is evident that the Roman Pontiff, enjoying the fullness of legislative and coercive power, is competent to use precept as an extrajudicial means of procedure. As lawgiver, the Pontiff is not bound beyond the demands of justice and equity in the punishment of crime and is not obligated to observe the formalities of the judicial or extrajudicial procedures. [1] Similarly, the universal legislative and coercive authority of the Ecumenical Council endows it with the power to impose precepts. Within the limits of

---

1 This follows from the converse of Wernz-Vidal's statement that "no prelate subordinate to the Roman Pontiff can punish without having issued a prior warning". *Ius Canonicum,* VII, 31.

their competency and with the approval of the Holy Father, the Sacred Congregations also are competent. [2]

Within their own competency, provincial and plenary councils also enjoy coercive powers. By their nature, it seems, they can make use of the extrajudicial process only during their sessions.

The common use of precept as a penal measure evidently rests with the immediate ecclesiastical superior, the local or religious ordinary. Thus, according to the norm of canon 2220, the local ordinary himself can impose precepts, the power being denied to the vicar general, unless he has a special mandate. [3]

The proper successor of the bishop, that is, the cathedral chapter, the board of diocesan consultors, the vicar capitular, or the diocesan administrator, possesses full jurisdiction including disciplinary and coercive powers. The apostolic administrator possesses jurisdiction according to the tenor of his appointment. Vicars and prefects apostolic, abbots and prelates *nullius* exercise ordinary jurisdiction over such territories respectively which have not yet been erected as dioceses or which have been exempted from the jurisdiction of residential bishops.

The metropolitan is limited in his exercise of coercive action to the time of visitation whch he has undertaken wth proper approval. He may punish notorious crimes perpetrated before his visitation, [4] or any open or notorious crime against himself or his entourage. In the Oriental Church, the patriarchs exercise coercive power since in this matter they truly enjoy jurisdiction. [5]

Among religious superiors, those who are ordinaries, namely, the abbot primate, abbots [6] of monastic congregations, abbots governing autonomous and independent

---

2 A case in point is found in the precept given by the Sacred Congregation of the Council to a priest of Sicily. The precept prohibited the use of the ecclesiastical garb and deprived this priest of all clerical rights and privileges of the sacred canons. - *AAS*, XXII (1930), 138. A precise and admirable study and listing of the competent ecclesiastical authorities is made in Esswein's *The Extrajudicial Coercive Powers of Ecclesiastical Superiors*, chapter 6, p. 51 ff. Cf. also Rainer, *Suspension of Clerics*, p. 113 ff.; Coronata, *Institutiones*, IV, p. 86 ff.

3 Cf. Lega-Bartoccetti, *Commentarius*, III, 197.

4 Canon 274, § 5.

5 Chelodi-Ciprotti, *De Delictis et Poenis*, p. 29.

6 Canon 198 and 488, § 8.

monasteries, supreme moderators, provincials and their vicars and those who possess similar powers, exercise full judicial and extrajudicial authority. The same faculty is enjoyed by the respective chapters associated with these superiors. [7]

Within a judicial trial, the *officialis,* the collegiate tribunal or a delegated judge is able to invoke sanctions, or to annex sanctions to their precepts - which are more properly termed "decrees" than precepts. [8]

The real problem arises on the question of local religious superiors of exempt clerical orders. According to the strict wording of the law these superiors are not major superiors and, as a consequence, lack both judicial and extrajudicial power. Canon 501, § 1 merely states that superiors and their chapters in exempt clerical institutes have ecclesiastical jurisdiction in the internal and external forums. Canon 2220, §1gives to those who have the power of imposing precepts the faculty of attaching sanctions to them. Inasmuch as a local superior enjoys full jurisdiction over his community, even though an imperfect one, it seems to many canonists that these superiors enjoy the faculty of attaching sanctions to their precepts. [9]

This question is thoroughly explored by Clancy in his dissertation on *The Local Religious Superior.* His conclusions are in harmony with the doctrine of Noval. Regulars who enjoy jurisdiction over an imperfect community possess the necessary extrajudicial power of inflicting penalties by way of precept. [10]

In his interpretation of the word *superiors* in canon 501, § 1 Clancy [11] teaches that the local superior is included under the general term and accordingly has jurisdiction in

---

7 Canon 501, § 1.

8 Cf. Esswein, *Extrajudicial Powers,* p. 71; Heylen, *De Censuris,* p. 39.

9 E.g., Noval, *De Iudiciis,* p. 498; Lega-Bartocetti, *Commentarius,* III, 197.

10 Noval, *De Iudiciis,* p. 498; Cf. also Lega-Bartoccetti, *Commentarius,* III, 197; Michiels, "De reservatione", *ETL,* IV (1927), 182; Wernz-Vidal, *Ius Canonicum,* VII, 31; Berutti, *Institutiones,* VI, 85; Raus, *Institutiones Canonicae,* 689-690.

11 *Op. cit.,* p. 28.

its fullness, unless the Code or the constitutions restrict this power. [12]

The ultimate source of the superior's right to issue precepts and inflict penalties extrajudicially is discovered in his legislative power. According to the Code the local superior is not an ordinary and as a consequence his lawmaking authority is not evident.

In proving the superior's right to make laws and to issue precepts, Clancy offers these reasons: [13] (1) if the concept of the common good is applied to the members of a religious house as a part of the Church, the commands of the superior fulfill this essential requirements; (2) there is nothing in the nature of the community to render the local superior incapable of passing a law for the members as parts of the perfect society and not only as parts of an imperfect society; (3) the present powers are capable of extension to include full legislative authority. [14]

The coercive power of the superior of an exempt clerical institute includes the ability to annex canonical penalties, including censures, to the precepts which he can give in virtue of his jurisdictional power. Since canon 501, § 1 recognizes the fundamental jurisdiction of the local superior, it must be concluded that the jurisdiction therein conceded extends to everything to which jurisdiction generally extends, unless some particular function is taken away from the local superior either by the common law or by his own constitutions.

There are no canons which explicitly or implicitly take away all coercive jurisdiction from the local superior. The local superior possesses no judicial authority and the extrajudicial procedures treated in canon 2186-2194 and 2301-2313 are restricted to ordinaries. Canon 2309, § 6 uses the term superiors but the context of the law shows that this also means ordinaries.

No canon explicitly states that the local superior can impose jurisdictional precepts. To this, Clancy replies that

12 Clancy *(op. cit.*, pp. 184-185) lists these authors as conceding power to local superiors: Claeys-Bouuaert — Simenon, O'Brien, Vermeersch, - Creusen, Noval, Fanfani, Coronata, Cerato, Cipollini, Ferreres, Crnica, Noldin - Schonegger. The power is denied by Cappello, Chelodi, Chelodi-Ciprotti, Salucci.

13 *Op. cit.*, pp. 42-44.

14 Ibid., pp. 181-183.

in order that the local superior be able to exercise any act of jurisdiction it is sufficient that particular act be not taken away or limited in the Code or constitutions. He continues that the superior's authority necessarily includes the right to command the actions of his subjects. Therefore the power to enforce these commands must likewise be given.

From canon 2220, § 1 alone, one must conclude, according to Clancy,[15] that the local superior can establish any penalty which can be in inflicted extrajudicially by way of precept. This would include both *latae* and *ferendae sententiae* penalties, since canon 1933, § 4 does not distinguish.

This interpretation, however, is confronted with other difficulties in other parts of the law which are not only not silent about the superior's authority but in matter of extrajudicial penalties positively restrict to the ordinary the right of inflicting them. Thus, canon 2233, § 2 states that no censure can be inflicted without a previous canonical warning and canon 2307 restricts this power to the ordinary. The difficulty is solved by Noval.[56] The local superior, whom Noval terms a non-ordinary with jurisdiction, can impose censures as an ordinary but only by way of precept, that is, he can threaten or inflict them as either *latae* or *ferendae sententiae* penalties by attaching them to the commands given to individual subjects. These penalties may be declared or inflicted only extrajudicially, in writing or orally before two witnesses. If the preceding superior had established the penalties by means of a document or before two witnesses, the succeeding superior may enforce them. The local superior cannot issue admonitions, reproofs, or other penal remedies or penances nor can he conduct any criminal investigations.

Although the superior is incapable of issuing a canonical admonition or the precept of canon 2310, nevertheless he can impose a precept which Noval terms a certain command or prohibition either with or without a penalty as accessory to the precept. Consequently, the superior is limited in his use of canon 1933, § 4, in applying its penalties only after he has constituted the penalty by way of a precept.

---

15 *Op. cit.*, pp. 192-193.

16 *De Iudiciis*, pp. 498-499.

ARTICLE 2. The Subject

The subject of ecclesiastical law or precept is defined in canon 2226, § 1. One is a subject of the local ordinary by holding a domicile or quasi-domicile within his territory. This binds the person not only to the observance of the laws but also to the precepts imposed directly upon him by the ordinary. By virtue of canon 24, precepts bind everywhere even outside the limits of the territory and can be imposed on a subject even though he be absent from the territory. The same binding force of and subjection to laws and precepts, in view of their actual physical presence in a territory, exists also for *vagi.*[17] Religious are bound to observe jurisdictional precepts of their religious superiors under pain of ecclesiastical penalties only when they are formally and completely subject to the jurisdiction of the exempt clerical institute and thereby removed from the jurisdiction of the local ordinary.

The question of change of domicile after the imposition of a precept affects the matter of subjection to the penalty threatened by the precept. The various aspects of this problem are discussed by Esswein[18] as follows:

> "After one has changed his domicile, if he commits a transgression that was prohibited under pain of censure by his former ecclesiastical superior, that superior cannot inflict or demand the observance of that censure... for through the change of domicile one ceases to be the subject of his former ecclesiastical superior, even as regards personal precept. If a precept, having annexed thereto a *ferendae sententiae* censure, is imposed upon a subject, the change of domicile or entrance into a religious Order before the imposition of the censure will free the transgressor of the liability of incurring it... If, however, a censure is conditionally inflicted with reference to something in the past which was done at a time when a domicile was had in the territory of the superior imposing the censure, then a change of domicile will not free a person from the liabili-

17 Esswein, *Extrajudicial Powers*, p. 74.

18 *Op. cit.*, p. 78.

ty of incurring the censure; thus, a superior may state: 'Unless you restore the stolen things within one month, you will be excommunicated', and then the change of domicile before the lapse of that time will not free the subject from the obligation imposed."

In regard to the Sacred Roman Congregations their subjects like other limits of their competency are determined in the law. Their territory or competency, unless defined, as for instance in the cases of the Sacred Congregation for the Oriental Church or of the Sacred Congregation for the Propagation of the Faith, is the whole world, since they serve and act in the name of the Holy Father, the supreme legislator.

By canon 1557, § 1 the right to judge supreme rulers, cardinals, legates and bishops is reserved to the Holy Father. The principle preserved here, namely of reserving judgment of their cases to the Pontiff himself, is applicable also to the extrajudicial process and so excludes these personages from punishment by way of precept imposed by the ordinary.[19]

The Code makes special provisions in naming those things in which religious are not exempt from the jurisdiction of the local ordinary. Thus, if an exempt religious commits a delict when absent from his convent, the local ordinary may proceed to the infliction of penal measures only after the proper superior has been notified.[20] If a religious is illegitimately absent from his convent, he is deprived of his privilege of exemption. The transgression may be inflicted immediately without reference to the religious superior.[21] In matters in which exempt religious are not removed from his jurisdiction, the ordinary possesses full jurisdiction and is able to enforce the common law even by means of precepts.[22] The local ordinary can use his extrajudicial power of precept: when there is an interference by the religious with the ordinary's right to pontificate and preach in exempt churches;[23] when they do not

19 Berutti, *Institutiones,* VI, 85.

20 Canon 616, § 2.

21 Canon 616, § 1.

2 The matters in which religious are not removed from the jurisdiction of the ordinary are listed by Esswein, *op. cit.,* p. 89 ff. and is presented here for completeness.

partake in the periodical conferences of the clergy as the law prescribes;[24] when they refuse submission and obedience to vicars and prefects apostolic in those things in which the Code makes them subject;[25] when the laws concerning the subjection of religious pastors to local ordinaries are not observed, as, for example, the regulations concerning prolonged absence of a pastor from his parish[26] when religious parochial vicars refuse to comply with the regulations of the local ordinary in regard to their legitimate removal;[27] when there is an interference with the rights of the local ordinary during the visitation of clerical congregations of pontifical approval, although these be exempt;[28] when the prescriptions of the local ordinary are not observed in regard to money received for parishes or missions;[29] when the notice of the approaching admission to the novitiate or to profession is not sent in spite of the local ordinary's demand;[30] when they refuse to correct abuses existent in cloister subject to the vigilance of the local ordinary[31] when they refuse to adapt themselves to the regulations of the local ordinary in the case in which the conducting of divine services in exempt churches interfers with parochial duties;[32] when they refuse to comply with the enactments of the local ordinary concerning the ringing of bells, the recitation of public prayers and the *"oratio imperata"*;[33] when they act in opposition to the rights of the local ordinary concerning the erection of third orders secular;[34] when there is interference with the ordinary's right to confirm even in exempt places;[35] when the prescriptions concerning the granting to transient priests, of permission to celebrate Mass are transgressed;[36] when the law concerning the determination of manual

---

23 Canons 337, § 1; 1343, § 1.

24 Canon 131, § 3.

25 Canons 295; 296; 297; 298; 307.

26 Canons 451, § 1; 454, § 5; 465, §§ 4, 5; 630, §§ 1, 2.

27 Canons 471, § 3; 472, 1°; 467, § 4; 477, § 1.

28 Canon 512, § 2, 2°.

29 Canon 533, § 1, 4°.

30 Canon 552, § 1.

31 Canon 603, § 1.

32 Canon 609, § 3.

33 Canon 612.

34 Canon 703, §§ 2, 3.

35 Canon 792.

36 Canon 804, § 3.

stipends is violated;[37] when delegation for the hearing of confessions, whether of the laity or of religious, is not sought from the local ordinary;[38] when the law concerning the promulgation of new indulgences is broken;[39] when the rights of the ordinary concerning the consecration or blessing of exempt places in his territory are denied him;[40] when public oratories or churches are erected without seeking the proper permission;[41] when prayers and exercises of piety are conducted in opposition to the regulations enacted by the local ordinary;[42] when the safeguards for divine worship and for the integrity of morals as prescribed by the local ordinary are not observed;[43] when the rules made to govern Benediction of the Blessed Sacrament are deliberately ignored;[44] when unusual pictures and images are publicly exposed in churches;[45] when relics without the proper authentication are exposed for veneration;[46] when public processions are conducted in defiance of the decrees of the local ordinary;[47] when a fee greater than that permitted by the bishop is demanded for the expenses incurred in the celebration of Holy Mass;[48] when a reasonable request of the local ordinary concerning assistance in matters of catechetical and religious instruction is refused;[49] when preaching is undertaken without a previous request for the proper authorization, or when the prescriptions of the local ordinary concerning preaching are ignored;[50] when legitimate contributions for the diocesan seminary are withheld, as also for other extraordinary diocesan assessments;[51] when the rights of the ordinary in the visitation of schools, asylums, hospitals and orphanages in matters of religious

---

37 Canon 831, § 3.
38 Canons 874; § 1; 876.
39 Canon 919, §1.
40 Canons 1155, § 1; 1157; 1169.
41 Canon 1162, § 1.
42 Canon 1259, § 1.
43 Canon 1261, § 2.
44 Canon 1274, § 1.
45 Canon 1279, § 1.
46 Canon 1283, § 1.
47 Canons 1291; 1292.
48 Canon 1303, § 3.
49 Canons 1334; 1336.
50 Canons 1338, §§ 2, 3; 1345.
51 Canons 1355; 1356; 1505.

and moral instruction are denied; [52] when the laws governing the publication of books, etc. are not observed; [53] when they refuse to make a profession of faith as required by the Code; [54] when they deny the competency of the local ordinary in controversies for which the Code declares the ordinary competent. [55]

---

52 Canons 1382; 1491.

53 Canons 1385, § 2; 1386, 1388.

54 Canon 1406, § 1, 7°.

55 Canon 1579.

CHAPTER SEVEN

INCIDENTAL QUESTIONS

The questions concerning whether penal precepts *a iure* or *ab homine,* the reservation of penalties inflicted by precept, and the matter of recourse against penal precepts are major problems which have been treated in detail in particular studies which have fully discussed their natures. A very brief summary of the doctrine of the canonists is offered here only for the sake of completeness.

ARTICLE 1. Whether Particular Penal Precepts are *a Iure* or *ab Homine*

> *Poena dicitur...* a iure, *si poena determinata in ipsa lege statuatur, sive latae sententiae sit sive ferendae;* ab homine, *si feratur per modum praecepti peculiaris...; quare poena ferendae sententiae, legi addita, ante sententiam condemnatorium est* a iure tantum, *postea a iure simul et* ab homine, *sed consideratur tanquam* ab homine.[1]

Concerning the designation of penal precepts as either *a iure* or *ab homine,* there are two opinions. The first claims that all penalties constituted or inflicted by way of a particular precept either *latae or ferendae sententiae* are *ab homine.* [2]

This follows the common doctrine of the pre-Code canonists. [3]

According to the other opinion all *latae sententiae* penalties attached to precepts are *a iure* and all *ferendae*

1 Canon 2217, § 1, n. 3.

2 The proponets of this opinion are Sole, Van Hove, Eichmann, Chelodi, Wernz-Vidal, Cappello, Berutti, Vermeerch-Creusen (in the 1928 edition of the *Epitome*). Cf. Onclin, *De Territoriali vel Personali Legis Indole,* pp. 365-366, note. Coronata adds the names of Wernz and D'Annibale—*Institutiones,* IV, p. 80, n. 4. Cf. also Cipollini, *De Censuris,* p. 7; Raus, *Institutiones Canonicae,* p. 697; Sipos, *Enchiridion,* p. 917.

3 Onclin, *op. cit.,* pp. 238, 307, 365.

sententiae penalties inflicted by precept are *ab homine.*[4] Although this contradicts the universal opinion of the pre-Code authors, it is a better interpretation of the Code, since it eliminates the seeming contradiction between paragraphs 2 and 4 of canon 2245 [5]

Perhaps the departure from pre-Code discipline is not so radical. The distinction between precepts *ad instar legis* and *ad instar sententiae* have been used throughout this study.[6] The terms seem similar to the older distinctions dividing precepts into those which constituted law and those which applied an already existing law,[7] or dividing precepts into those which were issued *per modum canonis* and those which were imposed *per modum sententiae.*[8] The former was considered as *a iure,* and the latter as *ab homine.*[9] From this the lines of the dispute are clearly defined as concerning *latae sententiae* precepts. The words of canon 2217, § 1, n. 3, *"si feratur per modum praecepti peculiaris",* certainly cover *ferendae sententiae* precepts. Therefore, a preventive *ferendae sententiae* precept is said to be *a iure* and the repressive precept both *a iure* and *ab homine* but is treated as *ab homine.*[10]

The conclusion of this discussion are important to the question of the reservation of particular *latae sententiae* precepts under the provisions of canon 2245, § 2 and § 4.

All particular penal precepts, according to the jurists who maintain the first opinion, are *ab homine.* The argument in support of this position is advanced by Beste in his

---

4 The canonists who support this opinion are Michiels, Tabera, Roberti, Morsdorf, Vermeersch-Creusen (1946 edition of *Epitome*) -Cf. Onclin, *op. cit.,* p. 366, n. 1. Coronata adds the names of Sipos and Cabreros de Anta to this list.- *Institutiones,* IV, p. 80, note 5. Coronata himself follows this opinion. Cf. also Rainer, *Suspension of Clerics,* pp. 49-51; Regatillo, *Institutiones,* II, 347; Bouscaren-Ellis, *Canon Law,* p. 803.

5 Other authors, to solve the seeming contradiction, have recourse to the common precept and claim that it is covered by canon 2245, § 4. The Code, however, omits all mention of common precepts. Cf. Onclin, *op. cit.,* p. 366.

6 Cf. p. 2, 20 ff., 43.

7 Cf. p. 2.

8 Hostiensis, *Commentaria* ad c. 21 (A nobis), X, *de sententia excommunicationis, suspensionis* et *interdicti,* V, 39.

9 Cipollini similarly distinguishes between precepts issued *per modum mandati* and those imposed *per modum sententiae.* Cf. *De Censuris, Latae Sententiae iuxta Codicem Iuris Canonici* (Taurini; Marietti, 1925), p. 7.

10 Cf. Cipollini, loc. cit.; Stadalnikas, *Reservation of Censures,* The Catholic University of America, Canon Law Studies, No. 208. (Washington, D. C.: The Catholic University of America Press, 1944), p. 94; Rainer, *Suspension of Clerics,* p. 50; Michiels, "De reservatione...," *ETL* IV (1927), 190-191.

discussion of the reservation of censures attached to particular precepts.[11] Since every particular precept is *ab homine,* they are reserved to the one who inflicted them.[12] However, no *latae sententiae* censure is reserved unless the reservation is stated expressly.[13] The comparison of canon 2217, § 1, no. 3, with canon 2245, § 2, certainly proves that every censure inflicted by way of precept is *ab homine.* The first part of paragraph 2 of the latter canon deals with censures *ab homine* while the remaining portion and the following paragraphs treat of censures *a iure.* The precept mentioned in paragraph 4, therefore, is understood as a common or a general precept. The principle that all particular precepts are *ab homine* is preserved by paragraph 2.

The interpretation of paragraph 4 as meaning common precept is in accord with pre-Code legislation,[14] and solves the seeming contradiction in canon 2245. The verb *"feratur"* of canon 2217, § 1, n. 3 comprehends the concepts of both the constitution and the infliction of penalties. The Code is not exact or discriminate in its choice of verbs to denote the concepts of the constitution and the infliction of penalties. Thus it uses *statuere, constituere, applicare, exsequi, declarare, decernere, irrogare,* as including the notion of *applicare* or *imponere.*[15]

It is admitted in the second opinion that the verb *feratur* is not definitely and solely restricted to the meaning of establishing and inflicting. But since the phrase *"per sententiam iudicialem"* is governed by the verb, the phrase *"per modum praecepti peculiaris"* should be understood in a similar manner as meaning the actual infliction or application of a penalty.[16] The Code, therefore, is speaking only of a precept *ad instar sententiae* and excluding precepts *ad*

---

11 *Introductio,* pp. 903-904.

12 Canon 2245, § 2, - *Censura* ab homine *est reservata ei qui censuram delegato; ex censuris vero* a iure *reservatis aliae sunt reservatae Ordinario, aliae* Apostolicae Sedis.

13 Canon 2245, § 4, - *Censura latae sententiae non est reservata, nisi in lege vel praecepto id express dicatur; et in dubio sive iuris sive facti reservatio non urget.*

14 Cf. also Onclin, *op. cit.,* p. 366; Sipos, *Enchiridion,* p. 908; Berutti, *Institutiones,* VI, 66-67.

15 Canons 2188, n. 2; 2220, § 2; 2225; 2231; 2236, § 1; 2244, § 3, etc. Cf. Rainer, *op. cit.,* p. 50. Note, however, that *infligatur* of canon 2225 is understood in this study as applying to both *latae* and *ferendae sententiae* penalties, and as connoting both the constitution and the imposition of penalties by way of precept.

16 Rainer, *op cit.,* p. 50; Michiels, "De reservatione...", *ETL,* IV (1927) 180, 613; Regatillo, *Institutiones, II,* 347.

instar iuris. A precept which threatens a *latae sententiae* penalty can hardly be said to inflict a penalty in the strict sense of inflict. Therefore such a penalty is simply *a iure* and not *ab homine.*

The jurisprudence on which this school bases its opinion is presented by Michiels.[17] Admittedly, at first sight canon 2217, § 1, n. 3, would include *latae sententiae* penalties under the wide sense of *feratur.* In addition, this opinion sees the contradiction which appears in the comparison with canon 2245, § 4, which states that a *latae sententiae* penalty can be reserved. This would seem to indicate that such a penalty could be regarded as *ab homine.*

A more detailed examination of both canons 2217, § 1, n. 3, and 2245, § 2 and § 4, however, supports the contention that only *ferendae sententiae* precepts are governed by canon 2217, § 1, n. 3. Here penalties *ab homine* are opposed to penalties *a iure* and *latae sententiae* penalties are opposed to *ferendae sententiae* penalties. In canon 2245, § 2 and § 4, the opposition exists between censures *ab homine* and censures *latae sententiae.* It seems, therefore, that *ab homine* censures imposed by way of precept must be regarded as meaning *ferendae sententiae* censures.

Paragraph 2 of canon 2217, § 1,[18] corroborates this. A *ferendae sententiae* penalty is said to be one which the judge or superior is called on to inflict *(infligi debeat).* Paragraph 3 defines an *ab homine* penalty *"si feratur per modum praecepti peculiaris."* The expression *ferendae sententiae* connotes the active subject inflicting the penalty while *ab homine* connotes the mode of the infliction.

As phrased in canon 2217, § 1, n. 3, the law seems inadequate in achieving the desired purpose. In defining *a iure* penalties as those determined in a law and *ab homine* penalties as those which are inflicted by way of a particular precept, it seems to omit mention of the *latae sententiae* penalties attached to precepts. Theoretically, however, this division regards the mode of the infliction of penalties. In *actu primo* both *latae* and *ferendae sententiae* penalties can derive *a iure.* In *actu secundo,* the actual imposition of

---

17 "De reservatione...", *ETL,* IV (1927), 180-194; 613-619.

18 Latae sententiae, *si poena determinata ita sit addita legi vel praecepto ut incurratur ipso facto commissi delicti;* ferendae sententiae, *si a iudice vel Superiore infligi debeat.*

ferendae sententiae penalties abstracts from the factors of law and precept, and are *ab homine; latae sententiae* penalties are exclsively *a iure.*

It is the conclusion of Michiel's study that it is morally certain that, according to the present legislation, *latae sententiae* penalties imposed by precept are not reserved, and, *a priori,* are not *ab homine.* The pre-Code discipline of considering all precepts as *ab homine* is abrogated, and canon 6, § 4°, does not furnish a rule of interpretation relative to penal precepts. Since the entire question is in doubt, there is no reservation attached to any *latae sententiae* penalty when express mention of reservation has not been made.

Though the law be lacking in precision, the private correction of the law is harmful and repugnant. Furthermore, there is no real conflict with the former law which was not incontestably certain. Canon 6, § 5°, applies to penal matters. The old penalties are abrogated by the Code, unless it appears certain they have been retained.

ARTICLE 2. The Reservation of Penalties Imposed by Way of Precept.

The preceding article has already indicated the doctrine concerning the reservation of censures. Obviously, it is within the right of the superior who imposes a *latae sententiae* precept to attach a reservation to the penalty. Reservation is odious as it increases the penalty. It should be used most sparingly and only in really grave delicts and when necessary for strengthening ecclesiastical discipline or extirpating vice from the conscience of the faithful. [19] If no mention is made of this reservation, the precept is *a iure* and is not reserved. In doubt, there is no reservation. [20]

Censures *ab homine* are reserved to the one who inflicted the censure or passed the sentence. [21] The superior

19 Canons 2246, § 1, and 897. Cf. Chelodi-Ciprotti, *De Delictis et Poenis,* p. 41.

20 Cf. Rainer, *Suspension of Clerics,* pp. 53-55; Regatillo, *Institutiones,* II, 364; Bouscaren-Ellis, *Canon Law,* p. 818; Chelodi-Ciprotti, *De Delictis et Poenis,* p. 41; Moriarty, *Extraordinary Absolution from Censures,* The Catholic University of America, Canon Law Studies, No. 113 (Washington, D. C.: The Catholic University of America, 1938), p. 91 sq.; Clancy, *The Local Religious Superior,* p. 195; Prümmer, *Manuale,* p. 654; Michiels, "De reservatione...", *ETL,* IV (1927), 618.

21 Canon 2245, § 2.

to whom the precept is reserved is the one who issued the precept, his superior, his successor or their delegate.[22] The successor of the one who imposed the precept is the one who succeeds to the same office, not the one who is the successor by reason of the subject's change of domicile or quasi-domicile. This latter superior cannot be the successor of the one who inflicted the censure, as is evident from the fact that the one who inflicted the censure can grant absolution even though the guilty one has changed his domicile.[23]

Reservations attached to precepts are reserved everywhere (ubique),[24] and hence continue in force for travellers.[25]

The declaratory sentence which states that a *latae sententiae* penalty has been incurred does not influence the reservation or non- reservation of the *latae sententiae* penalty and does not change an *a iure* penalty into an *ab homine* penalty.[26]

ARTICLE 3. Recourse Against Penal Precepts.

A subject on whom a precept, either preventive or repressive, has been imposed may feel himself agrieved. Hence, his right of recourse is recognized by the law in canon 2243, § 2. The law, however, does not furnish any guide for the complete procedure in these cases as it has provided for appealing from a sentence. A few points are evident. The recourse should be in writing and should be addressed to the proper superior of the one who inflicted the precept. Evidently there can be no recourse from the precepts of the Roman Pontiff, the supreme legislator. The usual case will be the recourse from the precepts of the ordinary or of the local superior of exempt clerical religious.

Although the Roman Pontiff has direct control over the extrajudicial acts of ordinaries, this authority is commonly exercised through one of the Sacred Congregations.

---

22 Michiels, "De reservatione..." *ETL*, IV (1927), 181-182; Rainer, *op. cit.* p. 52.

23 Chelodi-Ciprotti, *De Delictis et Poenis*, p. 41; Rainer, *loc. cit.*

24 Chelodi-Ciprotti, *loc. cit.;* Raus, *Institutiones Canonicae*, p. 697, note 1; Sipos, *Enchiridion*, p. 917.

25 Chelodi-Ciprotti, *loc. cit.*

26 Regatillo, *Institutiones*, II, 364; Moriarty, *Extraordinary Absolution from Censures*, p. 176.

Thus, the Sacred Congregation of the Council is competent to receive recourse against the administrative acts of the local ordinaries,[27] while the Sacred Congregation for the Affairs of Religious is competent to receive the recourse of religious against precepts of their superiors.[28] In mission countries, the Congregation for the Propagation of the Faith is competent.[29] Subjects pertaining to any of the Oriental rites are governed by the Sacred Congregation for the Oriental Church. This includes disputes in which a Latin Catholic may be involved. Thus a priest of an Oriental rite who is legitimately given a precept by a Latin ordinary should address his recourse to the Congregation for the Oriental Church.[30]

For the preservation of good order and discipline the superior should be notified of the recourse, especially if the matter be one which allows a suspensive effect.[31] Recourses with suspensive effect should be made within the time limits set for appeals, ten days.[32] Recourse against vindicative penalties is governed by canons 647, § 2, 4°; 1456, § 1; 2146 and 2153, § 1. Again the time limit is ten days. This norm may be used for the question of vindicative penalties inflicted by precept. The provision for the *tempus utile*[33] is also applicable to precepts.[34]

McClunn notes the difference regarding the effects of recourse against vindicative penalties and of recourse against censures. The former operates *in suspensivo.*[35]

The purpose of a censure being the correction of the delinquent, his welfare demands promptness. If the person admits the delict but considers the punishment too grave, his recourse is still *in devolutivo.* Vindicative penalties serve the purpose of expiating the delict and restoring the

---

27 Canon 250, § 1.

28 Canon 251, § 1.

29 Canon 252, § 3.

30 The doctrine governing recourse is taken liberally from McClunn, *Administrative Recourse,* The Catholic University of America Canon Law Studies, No. 240 (Washington, D. C.: The Catholic University of America Press, 1946), Chapter V, pp. 72 ff.

31 McClunn, *op. cit.,* p. 39.

32 Canon 1881. Cf. McClunn, *op. cit.,* pp. 51 ff.

33 Canon 35.

34 McClunn, *op. cit.* p. 66.

35 *Op. cit.,* p. 94; Cf. also Roberti, *De Delictis et Poenis,* Vol. I, pars 2, p. 301.

social order. Therefore, deferring the application of these penalties is not likely to bring damage or harm.

The effect of recourse against a precept which threatens a latae sententiae censure depends upon the matter of the precept.[36] If the matter does not admit of a suspensive recourse, the recourse will suspend neither the censure nor the precept.[37] If the law does not exclude a suspensive effect, the recourse is *in suspensivo.* If recourse is taken against the precept itself, there is no obligation to obey the precept. In a particular instance the recourse against the censure threatened by the precept may be *in suspensivo,* and yet the matter of the precept itself may not admit of a suspensive effect. Recourse in such a case would suspend the censure but not the obligation to obey.[38] Generally recourse has a non-suspensive effect when it is taken against the decree or precept or penalty of an ordinary or superior who has acted within the limits of his powers.[39] For example, recourse against a penalty inflicted according to canon 2225 would have a non-suspensive effect for the punishment has already been meted out.[40]

ARTICLE 4. *Miscellanea.*

What course of action is open to one who considers the precept imposed upon him as invalid and unjust with reference to the matter, the mode of infliction, or the authority of the superior?

If the precept is so excessive that the superior exceeded his power in giving it, the precept is invalid and its observance is not obligatory.[41] Coronata[42] shows some of the headings on which the precept may be invalid. Thus, the subject may not be contumacious or there may be lacking any delict or cause for the precept,[43] or the superior

---

36 Canon 2243, § 2.

37 Some canons do not admit of recourse *in suspensivo,* e.g. canons 106, 6°; 192, § 3; 296, § 2; 298; 345; 454, § 5; 513, § 2; 880, § 2; 1340, § 3; 1395, § 2; 142, § 3; 1465, § 1; 2146; 2287; etc.

38 Canon 2243, § 3.

39 Cf. Augustine, *Commentary,* VIII, 122-123; Roberti, *De Delictis et Poenis,* Vol. I, pars 2, p. 301; Blat, *De Delictis et Poenis,* p. 96; Morsdorf, *Rechtsprechung,* p. 167; Sipos, *Enchiridion,* p. 919.

40 Coronata, *Institutiones,* IV, 161.

41 McClunn, *Administrative Recourse,* p. 115.

42 *Institutiones,* IV, 161-162 text and note 1 on p. 162.

may lack jurisdiction. Even though the recourse against an invalid penalty may be denied and the precept confirmed, the censure does not bind if it is really unjust. Its observance, however, may indeed be necessary in order to avoid scandal and disruption of good order. If the justness of the inflicted censure is objectively doubtful and not merely subjectively so according to the aggrieved feelings of the subject, the censure should be observed like any other validly imposed penalty. If proper procedure has been followed, the presumption of justice would lie with the action of the superior.

CONCLUSIONS

1. The canonical penal precept has a twofold aspect, namely as a deterrent and as a penalty.

2. Canon 2310, with regard to the precept as a penal remedy or deterrent, canon 1933, § 4, with reference to the infliction of certain penalties by precept, and canon 2225, in relation to the form of the precept in the inflicting of a penalty, are all parts of one legal institute.

3. Canon 1933, § 4 contains an exhaustive list of the penalties which can be inflicted by precept when such penalties have been constituted by a prior precept.

4. Ordinarily a penal precept should be reduced to writing. A preventive precept should express the authority of the one imposing it, the subject, the command or prohibition under threat of penalty, the cause, the date, the place and seal, the signatures of the ordinary and the chancellor or a notary or of two witnesses. The subject may sign if he wishes. An authentic copy should be given or sent to the subject.

5. Preventive and repressive precepts are similar in form except as regards the cause. For a preventive precept the suspicion of actual wrongdoing or the danger of it is sufficient cause. For a repressive precept, the cause is the actual transgression of the preventive precept.

6. A *latae sententiae* penal precept is *a iure*. A *ferendae sententiae* penal precept is *ab homine*.

7. Unless it is so expressely stated in the precept, no *latae sententiae* penal precept is reserved.

8. The local religious superior of a house of exempt clerical religious is competent to use the extrajudicial procedure to issue preventive or repressive penal precepts.

BIBLIOGRAPHY

SOURCES

Acta et Decreta Concilii Plenarii Baltimorensis Tertii, A. D. MDCCCLXXXIV, Baltimorae: John Murphy, 1886.

Acta Sanctae Sedis, 41 vols., Romae, 1865-1908.

Codex Iuris Canonici Pii X Pontificis Maximi iussu digestus Benedicti Papae XV auctoritate promulgatus, Romae, Typis Polyglottis Vaticanis, 1917.

Bouscaren, T. L., *Canon Law Digest*, 2 vols., Milwaukee: Bruce, 1934-1943.

Codex Iuris Canonici Fontes, cura Emi Petri Card. Gasparri editi, 9 vols., Romae (postea Civitate Vaticana): Typis Polyglottis Vaticanis, 1923-1939. (Vols. VII-IX, ed. cura et studio Emi Iustiniani Card. Serédi.)

Collectanea in Usum Secretariae S. C. Episcoporum et Regularium, ed. A, Bizzarri, Romae, 1885.

Collectanea Sacrae Congregationis de Propaganda Fide, 2 vols., Romae, Typographia Polyglotta S. C. de Prop. Fide, 1907.

Corpus Iuris Canonici, ed. Lipsiensis 2, Aemilius L. Richter-Aemilius Friedberg, 2 vols., Lipsiae: Tauchanitz, 1879-1881. Editio anastatice repetita, 1928.

Decretales D. Gregorii Papae IX, una cum Glossis Restitutae, Romae, 1582.

Decretum Gratiani, Emendatum et Notationibus Illustratum una cum Glossis, Romae, 1582.

Jaffé, Phillipus, *Regesta Pontificum Romanorum ab condita Ecclesia ad annum post Christum natum MCXCVIII*, 2. ed. cura G. Wattenbach, S. Lowenfeld, F. Kaltenbrunner, P. Ewald, 2 vols. in 1, Lipsiae: Veit et Comp., 1885-1888.

Mansi, Joannes, *Sacrorum Conciliorum Nova et Amplissima Collectio*, 53 vols. in 60, Parisiis, 1901-1927.

Migne, Jacques Paul, *Patrologiae Cursus Completus series Latina,* 221 vols. Parisiis, 1844-1864.

Potthast, Augustus, *Regesta Pontificum Romanorum inde ab anno post Christum natum MCXCVIII ad annum MCCCIV,* 2 vols., Berolini, 1874-1875.

S. Romanae Rotae Decisiones seu sententiae quae prodierunt ab anno 1909, 32 vols., 1909-1940 inclusive, Romae, 1912-

REFERENCE WORKS

Augustine, Charles, *A Commentary on the New Code of Canon Law,* 8 vols., Vol. VIII, St. Louis; Herder, 1922.

Ayrinhac, H. A.-Lydon, J. P., *Penal Legislation in the Code of Canon Law,* revised edition, New York: Benziger, Brothers, 1944.

Benedictus XIV, Pont. Opt. Max., olim Prosper Cardinalis de Lambertinis, *De Synodo Dioecesana,* 2. ed., 2 vols., Parmae, 1764

Berutti, Christopher, *Institutiones Iuris Canonici,* 5 vols., Taurini: Marietti, 1936-1943.

Beste, Udalricus, *Introductio in Codicem,* ed. altera, Collegeville, Minn., St. John's Abbey Press, 1934.

Blat, Albert, *Commentarium Textus Codicis Iuris Canonici,* Liber IV, *Tractatus De Processibus,* Romae: Collegio "Angelico", 1927. Liber V, *De Delictis et Poenis,* Romae: Collegio "Angelico", 1942.

Bouix, *De Judiciis Ecclesiasticis*, 3. ed., 2 vols., Parisiis, 1885.

Bouscaren, T. L-Ellis, A. C., *Canon Law, A Text and Commentary,* Milwaukee: Bruce, 1946.

Cappello, Felix M., *Tractatus Canonico-moralis de Censuris,* 2 ed., Turinorum Augustae: Marietti, 1925.
Summa Iuris Canonici, 3 vols., Vol. III, Romae: Apud Aedes Universitatis Gregorianae, 1936.

Casey, James V., *A Study of Canon 2222, § 1,* The Catholic University of America Canon Law Studies, No. 290, Washington, D. C.: The Catholic University of America Press, 1949.

Chelodi, Ioannes, *Ius Poenale,* 3 ed. Tridenti, 1933.

Chelodi, Ioannes, et Ciprotti, Pius, *Ius Canonicum, De Delictis et Poenis et de Iudiciis Criminalibus,* 5. ed., Vicenza: Societa Anonima Typografica, 1943.

Cicognani, Amleto, *Canon Law,* 2nd revised edition, English version by J. O'Hara and F. Brennan, Westminster, Md.: Newman Bookshop, 1946.

Cipollini, Albertus, *De Censuris,* Latae Sententiae juxta Codicem Iuris Canonici, Taurini; Marietti, 1925.

Clancy, Patrick, *The Local Religious Superior,* The Catholic University of America Canon Law Studies, No. 175, Washington, D. C.: The Catholic University of America Press, 1943.

Cocchi, Guidus, *Commentarium in Codicem Iuris Canonici,* 8 vols. in 5, Vol. VIII, 4. ed., Taurinorum Augustae: Marietti, 1938.

Coronata, Matthaeus Conte A, *Institutiones Iuris Canonici,* 2 ed. 5 vols., Taurini: Marietti, 1939-1947.

De Meester, A., *Juris Canonici et Juris Canonico-civilis Compendium,* nova editio, 3 vols. in 4, Brugis: Desclée de Brouwer et Sii, 1921-1928.

Droste, Francis - Messmer, Sebastian G., *Canonical Procedure in Disciplinary and Criminal Causes of Clerics,* New York, 1897.

Durandus, Gulielmus, *Speculum Iuris,* Venetiis, 1677.

Esswein, Anthony A., *The Extrajudicial Coercive Powers of Ecclesiastical Supeirors,* The Catholic University of America Canon Law Studies, No. 127, Washington, D. C.: The Catholic University of America Press, 1941.

Ferraris, Lucius, *Prompta Biblioteca Canonica, Iuridica, Moralis, Theologica, necnon Ascetica, Polemica, Rubristica, Historica, 9 vols., Romae, 1885-1899.*

Heylen, V, *De Censuris,* 4. ed., Mechliniae: H. Dessain, 1945.

Hostiensis, Cardinalis (Henricus de Segusio), *Commentaria in Quinque Decretalium Libros,* 5 vols., Venetiis, 1581.

————, *Summa Aurea,* Venetiis, 1570.

Lega, Michael, *Praelectiones in Textum Iuris Canonici: De Iudiciis Ecclesiasticis,* 4 vols., Romae, 1896-1901.

Lega, Michael Cardinalis, et Bartoccetti, Victorius, *Commentarius in Iudicia Ecclesiastica,* 3 vols., Romae: Anonima Libraria Cattolica Italiana, 1938-1941.

Makée, Ch. *Institutiones Iuris Ecclesiastici tum Publici tum Privati,* Tomus II, Parisiis, 1897.

Maroto, P., *Institutiones Iuris Canonici ad Normam Novi Codicis,* 2 vols., Vol. I, 2. ed., Matriti (Madrid), 1919.

McClunn, Justin, *Adiministrative Recourse,* The Catholic University of America Canon Law Studies No. 240, Washington D. C.: The Catholic University of America Press, 1946.

Meehan, Andreas B., *Compendium Iuris Canonici,* Roffae, 1899.

Moriarty, Francis E., *The Extraordinary Absolution from Censures,* The Catholic University of America Canon Law Studies No. 113, Washington, D. C.: The Catholic University of America, 1938.

Morsdorf, Klaus, *Rechtsprechung und Verwaltung in kanonischen Recht,* Freiburgi. Br.: Herder, 1941

Muñiz, Tomás, *Procedimientos Eclesiásticos,* 2. ed., 3 vols., Sevilla: Imp. y Lib. de Sabrino de Izquierdo, 1925

Noval, Joseph, *Commentarium Codicis Iuris Canonici,* Liber IV *De Processibus,* Pars I, *De Iudiciis,* Romae: Marietti, 1920.

O'Brien, Romaeus, *The Provincial Religious Superior,* The Catholic University of America Canon Law Studies No. 258, Washington, D. C.: The Catholic University of America Press, 1947.

O'Donnell, Cletus, *The Marriage of Minors,* The Catholic University of America Canon Law Studies No. 221, Washington, D. C.: The Catholic University of America Press, 1945.

Onclin, Gulielmo, *De Territoriali vel Personali Legis Indola,* Gemblaci: J. Duculat, 1938.

Panormitanus, Abbas (Nicholaus de Tudeschis), *Commentaria in Quinque Libros Decretalium,* 5 vols. in 7, Venetiis, 1588.

Passerinus, P. M., *Commentaria in I, II, et III Libri Sexti Decretalium,* Venetiis, 1698.

Periés, G., *La Procédure Canonique Moderne dans les Causes Discilinaires et Criminelles,* Paris, 1898.

Pierantonelli, Pacificus, *Praxis Fori Ecclesiastici ad Praesentem Ecclesiae Conditionem Accomodata,* Romae, 1883.

Prümer, Dominicus, *Manuale Iuris Canonici,* 4. et 5. ed., Freiburgi Brisgoviae: Herder & Co., 1927.

Rainer, Eligius, *Suspension of Clerics,* The Catholic University of America Canon Law Studies, No. 111, Washington, D. C.: The Catholic University of America, 1937.

Raus, J. B., *Institutiones Canonicae,* ed. altera, Lugduni: E. Vitte, 1931.

Regatillo, Eduardus, *Institutiones Iuris Canonici,* 2 vols., Santander; Sal Terrae, 1941-1942.

Roberti, Franciscus, *De Delictis et Poenis, De Delictis in Genere,* Vol. I, pars 1, 1930; Vol. I, pars 2, 1938, Romae, Apud Aedes Facultatis Iuridicae ad S. Apollinaris.

Romani, Sylvius, *Summa Juris Canonici Lineamenta,* Romae; Apud Auctorem, 1939.

Rota, Petrus, *Enchiridion Confessarii et Iudicis Ecclesiastici,* Taurini, 1884.

Sanguinetti, Sebastianus, *Iuris Ecclesiastici Privati Institutiones,* 3. ed., Romae, 1896.

Schmalzgrueber, Franciscus, *Jus Ecclesiasticum Universum,* 5 vols. in 12, Romae 1843-1845.

Sipos, Stephanus, *Enchiridion Iuris Canonici,* Pécs; Ex Typographia "Haladas R. T.", 1926.

Smith, S. B., *Elements of Ecclesiastical Law,* Vol. II *Ecclesiastical Trials,* 5. ed. New York, 1892.

———, *New Procedure in Criminal and Disciplinary Causes of Ecclesiastics in the United States,* 2. ed., New York: F. Pustet & Co., 1888.

Sole, Jacobus, *De Delictis et Poenis,* Romae, 1920.

Stadalnikas, Casimir, *Reservation of Censures,* The Catholic University of America Canon Law Studies, No. 208, Washington, D. C.: The Catholic University of America Press, 1944.

Suarez, Franciscus, *Opera Omnia,* 28 vols., ed. a C. Berton, Parisiis, 1856-1861.

Vermeersch, A. et Creusen, J., *Epitome Iuris Canonici,* 6. ed., 3 vols., Romae: H. Dessain, 1937-1946.

Wernz, F. X. et Vidal, Petrus, *Ius Canonicum,* 7 vols. in 8, Vol I and Vol. VII, Romae: Apud Aedes Universitatis gregorianae, 1937-1938.

Wernz, Franciscus, *Ius Decretalium,* 2. ed., 6 vols., Romae et Prati, 1906-1913.

Woywod, Stanislaus, *A Practical Commentary on the Code of Canon Law,* revised edition by Callistus Smith, New York: Joseph F. Wagner, 1946.

ARTICLES

Anonymous, "Procédure canonique," *Analecta Juris Pontificii,* XIX (1880), col. 1115-1129,

Cappello, Felix, "Iirrogatio poenae per modum praecepti extra iudicium", *Periodica,* XIX (1930), 36*-38*.

Michiels, G., "De reservatione censurae latae sententiae pracepto peculiari adnexae," *Ephemerides Theologicae Lovaniensis* IV (1927), 180-194; 613-619.

Noval, Joseph, "De ratione corrigendi et puniendi sive in iudicio sive extra iudicium iure Codicis I.C."—*Jus Pontificium,* I-II (1921-1922), 147-156; (1923), 36-40; 204-210.

Roberti, Franciscus, "Quaenam poenae applicari possint per modum praecepti?" *Apollinaris,* IV (1931), 294-300.

PERIODICALS

Analecta Juris Pontificii, 26 vols., Romae, 1855-1869; Parisiis, 1872-1891.

Apollinaris, Romae, 1928-

Ephemerides Theologicae Lovanienses, Lovanii, 1924—

Jus Pontificium, Romae 1921-1940.

Periodica de Re Canonica et Morali Utilia praesertim Religiosis et Missionariis, Brugis, 1905-

ABBREVIATIONS

AAS—*Acta Apostolicae Sedis.*

AJP—*Analecta Juris Pontificii.*

ASS—*Acta Sanctae Sedis.*

ETL—*Ephemerides Theologicae Lovanienses.*

Fontes—*Codicis Iuris Canonici Fontes* cura... Gasparri editi.

Jaffé—*Regesta Pontificum Romanorum ad annum 1198.*

JP—*Jus Pontificium.*

Mansi—*Sacrorum Conciliorum Nova et Amplissima Collectio.*

MPL—Migne, *Patrologia Latina.*

Periodica—*Periodica de Re Canonica et Morali Utilia praesertim Religiosis et Missionariis.*

Potthast—*Regesta Pontificum Romanorum ab anno 1198 ad annum 1304.*

S.R.R. Decis.—*S. Romanae Rotae Decisiones seu Sententiae.*

ALPHABETICAL INDEX

BIOGRAPHICAL NOTE

Hugh Gabriel Quinn was born January 1, 1915, in The Bronx, New York. He attended the parochial schools of St. Rita of Cascia in The Bronx and of St. Gerard Majella, Hollis, New York. He attended high school at Santa-Maria-on-Hudson, West Park, New York, where he also received Normal School Training. He then taught in various elementary and secondary schools in and around the City of New York. From September 1940 to June 1942 he studied scholastic philosophy at St. Joseph's College, Somerset, Ohio, receiving the degree of Bachelor of Arts on June 1, 1942. He subsequently studied Sacred Theology at St. Meinrad's Seminary, St. Meinrad, Indiana, and at the Theological College of the Catholic University of America, Washington, D. C., being ordained to the Holy Priesthood on June 15, 1946. In September, 1946, he enrolled in the School of Canon Law of the Catholic University of America, where he received the Degree of the Baccalaureate in Canon Law in June, 1947, and the Degree of the Licentiate in Canon Law in June, 1948.

CANON LAW STUDIES*

1. FRERIKS, REV. CELESTINE A., C.PP.S., J.C.D., Religious Congregations in Their External Relations, 121 pp. 1916.
2. GALLIHER, REV. DANIEL M., O.P., J.C.D., Canonical Elections, 117 pp., 1917.
3. BORKOWSKI, REV. AURELIUS L., O.F.M., J.C.D., De Confraternibus Ecclesiasticis, 136 pp., 1918.
4. CASTILLO, REV. CAYO, J.C.D., Disertación Histórico-Canónica sobre la Potestad del Cabildo en Sede Vacante o Impedida del Vicario Capitular, 99 pp., 1919 (1918).
5. KUBELBECK, REV. WILLIAM J., S.T.B., J.C.D., The Sacred Penitentiaria and its Relation to Faculties of Ordinaries and Priests. 129 pp., 1918.
6. PETROVITS, REV. JOSEPH, J.C., S.T.D., J.C.D., The New Church Law on Matrimony, X-461 pp., 1919.
7. HICKEY, REV. JOHN J., S.T.B., J.C.D., Irregularities and Simple Impediments in the New Code of Canon Law, 100 pp., 1920.
8. KLEKOTKA, REV. PETER J., S.T.B., J.C.D., Diocesan Consultors, 179 pp., 1920.
9. WANENMACHER, REV. FRANCIS, J.C.D., The Evidence in Ecclesiastical Procedure Affecting the Marriage Bond, 1920 (Printed 1935).
10. GOLDEN, REV. HENRY FRANCIS, J.C.D., Parochial Benefices in the New Code, IV-119 pp., 1921 (Printed 1925).
11. KOUDELKA, REV. CHARLES J., J.C.D., Pastors, Their Rights and Duties According to the New Code of Canon Law, 211 pp., 1921.
12. MELO, REV. ANTONIUS, O.F.M., J.C.D., De Exemptione Regularium, X-188 pp., 1921.
13. SCHAAF, REV. VALENTINE THEODORE, O.F.M., S.T.B., J.C.D., The Cloister, X-180 pp., 1921.
14. BURKE, REV. THOMAS JOSEPH, S.T.D., J.C.D., Competence in Ecclesiastical Tribunals, IV-117 pp., 1922.
15. LEECH, REV. GEORGE LEO, J.C.D., A Comparative Study of the Constitution "Apostolicae Sedis" and the "Codex Juris Canonici," 179 pp., 1922.
16. MOTRY, REV. HUBERT LOUIS, S.T.D., J.C.D., Diocesan Faculties According to the Code of Canon Law, II-167 pp., 1922.

---

* All published numbers are available from the Catholic University of America Press, 620 Michigan Avenue, N.E., Washington 17, D. C., except the following: Nos. 1-114 inclusive, 116, 118, 120, 121, 122, 123, 136, 153, 162, 182, and 198. But the following numbers, now reissued, are obtainable from *The Jurist*, The Catholic University of America, Washington 17, D. C., namely: Nos. 5, 7, 11, 17, 18, 19, 26, 28, 30, 31, 34, 42, 44, 51, 52 and 61.

17. MURPHY, REV. GEORGE LAWRENCE, J.C.D., Delinquencies and Penalties in the Administration and the Reception of the Sacraments, IV-121 pp. 1923.
18. O'REILLY, REV. JOHN ANTHONY, S.T.B., J.C.D., Ecclesiastical Sepulture in the New Code of Canon Law, II-129 pp., 1923.
19. MICHALICKA, REV. WENCESLAS CYRILL, O.S.B., J.C.D., Judicial Procedure in Dismissal or Clerical Exempt Religious, 107 pp., 1923.
20. DARGIN, REV. EDWARD VINCENT, S.T.B., J.C.D., Reserved Cases According to the Code of Canon Law, IV-103 pp., 1924.
21. GODFREY, REV. JOHN A., S.T.B., J.C.D., The Right of Patronage According to the Code of Canon Law, 153 pp., 1924.
22. HAGEDORN, REV. FRANCIS EDWARD, J.C.D., General Legislation on Indulgences, II-154 pp., 1924.
23. KING, REV. JAMES IGNATIUS, J.C.D., The Administration of the Sacraments to Dying Non-Catholics, V-141 pp., 1924.
24. WINSLOW, REV. FRANCIS JOSEPH, O.F.M., J.C.D., Vicars and Prefects Apostolic, IV-149 pp., 1924.
25. CORREA, REV. JOSE SERVELION, S.T.L., J.C.D., La Potestad Legislativa de la Iglesia Católica, IV-127 pp., 1925.
26. DUGAN, REV. HENRY FRANCIS, A.M., J.C.D., The Judiciary Department of the Diocesan Curia, 87 pp., 1925.
27. KELLER, REV. CHARLES FREDERICK, S.T.B., J.C.D., Mass Stipends, 167 pp., 1925.
28. PASCHANG, REV. JOHN LINUS, J.C.D., The Sacramentals According to the Code of Canon Law, 129 pp., 1925.
29. PIONTEK, REV. CYRILUS, O.F.M., S.T.B., J.C.D., De Indulto Exclaustrationis necnon Saecularizationis, XIII-289 pp., 1925.
30. KEARNEY, REV. RICHARD JOSEPH, S.T.B., J.C.D., Sponsors of Baptism According to the Code of Canon Law, IV-127 pp., 1925.
31. BARTLETT, REV. CHESTER JOSEPH, A.M., LL.B., J.C.D., The Tenure of Parochial Property in the United States of America, V-108 pp., 1926.
32. KILKER, REV. ADRIAN JEROME, J. C. D., Extreme Unction, V-425 pp., 1926.
33. McCORMICK, REV. ROBERT EMMETT, J. C. D., Confessors of Religious, VIII-266 pp., 1926.
34. MILLER, REV. NEWTON THOMAS, J.C.D., Founded Masses According to the Code of Canon Law, VII-93 pp., 1926.
35. ROELKER, REV. EDWARD G., S.T.D., J.C.D., Principles of Privilege According to the Code of Canon Law, XI-166 pp., 1926.

36. BAKALARCZYK, REV. RICHARDUS, M.I.C., J.U.D., De Novitiatu, VIII-208 pp., 1927.
37. PIZZUTI, REV. LAWRENCE, O.F.M., J.U.L., De Parochis Religiosis, 1927. (Not Printed).
38. BLILLEY, REV. NICHOLAS MARTIN, O.S.B., J.C.D., Altars According to the Code of Canon Law, XIX-132 pp., 1927.
39. BROWN, MR. BRENDAN FRANCIS, A.B., LL.M., J.U.D., The Canonical Juristic Personality with Special Reference to its Status in the United States of America, V-212 pp., 1927.
40. CAVANAUGH, REV. WILLIAM THOMAS, C.P., J.U.D., The Reservation of the Blessed Sacrament, VIII-101 pp., 1927.
41. DOHENY, REV. WILLIAM J., C.S.C., A.B., J.C.D., Church Property: Modes of Acquisition, X-118 pp., 1927.
42. FELDHAUS, REV. ALOYSIUS H., C.PP.S., J.C.D., Oratories, IV-141 pp., 1927.
43. KELLY, REV. JAMES PATRICK, A.B., J.C.D., The Jurisdiction of the Simple Confessor, X-208 pp., 1927.
44. NEUBERGER, REV. NICHOLAS J., J.C.D., Canon 6 or the Relation of the Codex Iuris Canonici to the Preceding Legislation, V-95 pp., 1927.
45. O'KEEFE, REV. GERALD MICHAEL, J.C.D., Matrimonial Dispensations, Powers of Bishops, Priests, and Confessors, VIII-232 pp., 1927.
46. QUIGLEY, REV. JOSEPH A. M., A.B., J.C.D., Condemned Societies, 139 pp., 1927.
47. ZAPLOTMIK, REV. JOHANNES LEO, J.C.D., De Vicariis Foraneis, X-142 pp., 1927.
48. DUSKIE, REV. JOHN ALOYSIUS, A.B., J.C.D., The Canonical Status of the Orientals in the United States, VIII-196 pp., 1928.
49. HYLAND, REV. FRANCIS EDWARD, J.C.D., Excommunication, Its Nature, Historical Development and Effects, VIII-181 pp., 1928.
50. REIMANN, REV. GERALD JOSEPH, O.M.C., J.C.D., The Third Order Secular of Saint Francis, 201 pp., 1928.
51. SCHENK, REV. FRANCIS J., J.C.D., The Matrimonial Impediments of Mixed Religion and Disparity of Cult, XVI-318 pp., 1929.
52. COADY, REV. JOHN JOSEPH, S.T.D., J.U.D., A.M., The Appointment of Pastors, VIII-150 pp., 1929.
53. KAY, REV. THOMAS HENRY, J.C.D., Competence in Matrimonial Procedure, VIII-164 pp., 1929.
54. TURNER, REV. SIDNEY JOSEPH, C.P., J.U., D., The Vow of Poverty, XLIX-217 pp., 1929.

55. KEARNEY, REV. RAYMOND A., A.B., S.T.D., J.C.D., The Principles of Delegation, VII-149 pp., 1929.
56. CONRAM, REV. EDWARD JAMES, A.B., J.C.D., The Interdict, V-163 pp., 1930.
57. O'NEILL, REV. WILLIAM H., J.C.D., Papal Rescripts of Favor, VII-218 pp., 1930.
58. BASTNAGEL, REV. CLEMENT VINCENT, J.U.D., The Appointment of Parochial Adjutants and Assistants, XV-257 pp., 1930.
59. FERRY, REV. WILLIAM A., A.B., J.C.D., Stole Fees, V-136 pp., 1930.
60. COSTELLO, REV. JOHN MICHAEL, A.B., J.C.D., Domicile and Quasi-Domicile, VII-201 pp., 1930.
61. KREMER, REV. MICHAEL NICHOLAS, A.B., S.T.B., J.C.D., Church Support in the United States, VI-136 pp., 1930.
62. ANGULO, REV. LUIS, C.M., J.C.D., Legislation de la Iglesia sobre la intencion en la application de la Santa Misa, VII-104 pp., 1931.
63. FREY, REV. WOLFGANG NORBERT, O.S.B., A.B., J.C.D., The Act of Religious Profession, VIII-174 pp., 1931.
64. ROBERTS, REV. JAMES BRENDAN, A.B., J.C.D., The Banns of Marriage, XIV-140 pp., 1931.
65. RYDER, REV. RAYMOND ALOYSIUS, A.B., J.C.D., Simony, IX-151 pp., 1931.
66. CAMPAGNA, REV. ANGELO, PH. D., J.U.D., Il Vicario Generale del Vescovo, VII-205 pp., 1931.
67. COX, REV. JOSEPH GODFREY, A.B., J.C.D., The Administration of Seminaries, VI-124 pp., 1931.
68. GREGORY, REV. DONALD J., J.U.D., The Pauline Privilege, XV-165 pp., 1931.
69. DONOHUE, REV. JOHN F., J.C.D., The Impediment of Crime, VII-110 pp., 1931.
70. DOOLEY, REV. EUGENE A., O.M.I., J.C.D., Church Law on Sacred Relics, IX-143 pp. 1931.
71. ORTH, REV. CLEMENT RAYMOND, O.M.C., J.C.D., The Approbation of Religious Institutes, 171 pp., 1931.
72. PERNICONE, REV. JOSEPH M., A.B., J.C.D., The Ecclesiastical Prohibitions of Books, XII-267 pp., 1932.
73. CLINTON, REV. CONNELL, A.B., J.C.D., The Paschal Precept, IX-108 pp., 1932.
74. DONNELLY, REV. FRANCIS B., A.M., S.T.L., J.C.D., The Diocesan Synod, VIII-125 pp., 1932.
75. TORRENTE, REV. CAMILO, C.M.F., J.C.D., Las Procesiones Sagradas, V-145 pp., 1932.

76. MURPHY, REV. EDWIN J., C.PP.S., J.C.D., Suspension Ex-Informata Conscientia, XI-122 pp., 1932.
77. MACKENSIE, REV. ERIC F., A.M., S.T.L., J.C.D., The Delict of Heresy in its Commission, Penalization, Absolution, VII-124 pp., 1932.
78. LYONS, REV. AVITUS E., S.T.B., J.C.D., The Collegiate Tribunal of First Instance, XI-147 pp., 1932.
79. CONNOLLY, REV. THOMAS A., J.C.D., Appeals, XI-195 pp., 1932.
80. SANGMEISTER, REV. JOSEPH V., A.B., J.C.D., Force and Fear as Precluding Matrimonial Consent, V-211 pp., 1932.
81. JAEGER, REV. LEO A., A.B., J.C.D., The Administration of Vacant and Quasi-Vacant Episcopal Sees in the United States, IX-229 pp., 1932.
82. RIMLINGER, REV. HERBERT T., J.C.D., Error Invalidating Matrimonial Consent, VII-79 pp., 1932.
83. BARRETT, REV. JOHN D. M., S.S., J.C.D., A Comparative Study of the Councils of Baltimore and the Code of Canon Law, IX-223 pp., 1932.
84. CARBERRY, REV. JOHN J., Ph.D., S.T.D., J.C.D., The Juridical Form of Marriage, X-177 pp., 1934.
85. DOLAN, REV. JOHN L., A.B., J.C.D., The Defensor Vinculi, XII-157 pp., 1934.
86. HANNAN, REV. JEROME D., A.M., S.T.D., LL.B., J.C.D., The Canon Law of Wills, IX-517 pp., 1934.
87. LEMIEUX, REV. DELISE A., A.M., J.C.D., The Sentence in Ecclesiastical Procedure, IX-131 pp., 1934.
88. O'ROURKE, REV. JAMES J., A.B., J.C.D., Parish Registers, VII-109 pp., 1934.
89. TIMLIN, REV. BARTHOLOMEW, O.F.M., A.M., J.C.D., Conditional Matrimonial Consent, X-381 pp., 1934.
90. WAHL, REV. FRANCIS X., A.B., J.C.D., The Matrimonial Impediments of Consanguinity and Affinity, VI-125 pp., 1934.
91. WHITE, REV. ROBERT J., A.B., LL.B., S.T.B., J.C.D., Canonical Ante-Nuptial Promises and the Civil Law, VI-152 pp., 1934.
92. HERRERA, REV. ANTONIO PARRA, O.C.D., J.C.D., Legislación Ecclesiastica sobre el Ayuno y la Abstinencia, IX-191 pp., 1935.
93. KENNEDY, REV. EDWIN J., J.C.D., The Special Matrimonial Process in Cases of Evident Nullity, X-165 pp., 1935.
94. MANNING, REV. JOHN J., A.B., J.C.D., Presumption of Law in Matrimonial Procedure, XI-111 pp., 1935.
95. MOEDER, REV. JOHN M., J.C.D., The Proper Bishop for Ordination and Dismissorial Letters, VII-135 pp., 1935.

96. O'MARA, REV. WILLIAM A., A.B., J.C.D., Canonical Causes for Matrimonial Dispensations, IX-155 pp., 1935.
97. REILLY, REV. PETER, J.C.D., Residence of Pastors, IX-81 pp., 1935.
98. SMITH, REV. MARINER T., O.P., S.T.Lr., J.C.D., The Penal Law for Religious, VIII-169 pp., 1935.
99. WHALEN, REV. DONALD W., A.M., J.C.D., The Value of Testimonial Evidence in Matrimonial Procedure, XIII-297 pp., 1935.
100. CLEARY, REV. JOSEPH F., Canonical Limitations on the Alienation of Church Property, VIII-141 pp., 1936.
101. GLYNN, REV. JOHN C., J.C.D., The Promotor of Justice, XX-337 pp., 1939.
102. BRENNAN, REV. JAMES H., S.S., M.A., S.T.B., J.C.D., The Simple Convalidation of Marriage, VI-135 pp., 1937.
103. BRUNINI, REV. JOSEPH BERNARD, J.C.D., The Clerical Obligations of Canons 139 and 142, X-121 pp., 1937.
104. CONNOR, REV. MAURICE, A.B., J.C.D., The Administrative Removal of Pastors, VIII-159 pp., 1937.
105. GUILFOYLE, REV. MERLIN JOSEPH, J.C.D., Custom, XI-144 pp., 1937.
106. HUGHES, REV. JAMES AUSTIN, A.B., A.M., J.C.D., Witnesses in Criminal Trials of Clerics, IX-140 pp., 1937.
107. JANSEN, REV. RAYMOND J., A.B., S.T.L., J.C.D., Canonical Provisions for Catechetical Instruction, VII-153 pp., 1937.
108. KEALY, REV. JOHN JAMES, A.B., J.C.D., The Introductory Libellus in Church Court Procedure, XI-121 pp., 1937.
109. McMANUS, REV. JAMES EDWARD, C.SS.R., J.C.D., The Administration of Temporal Goods in Religious Institutes, XVI-196 pp., 1937.
110. MORIARTY, REV. EUGENE JAMES, J.C.D., Oaths in Ecclesiastical Courts X-115 pp., 1937.
111. RAINER, REV. ELIGIUS GEORGE, C.SS.R., J.C.D., Suspension of Clerics, XVII-249 pp., 1937.
112. REILLY, REV. THOMAS F., C.SS.R., J.C.D., Visitation of Religious, VI-195 pp., 1938.
113. MORIARTY, REV. FRANCIS E., C.SS.R., J.C.D., The Extraordinary Absolution from Censures, XV-334 pp., 1938.
114. CONNOLLY, REV. NICHOLAS P., J.C.D., The Canonical Erection of Parishes, X-132 pp., 1938.
115. DONOVAN, REV. JAMES JOSEPH, J.C.D., The Pastor's Obligation in Prenuptial Investigation, XII-322 pp., 1938.
116. HARRIGAN, REV. ROBERT J., M.A., S.T.B., J.C.D., The Radical Sanation of Invalid Marriages, VIII-208 pp., 1938.

117. BOFFA, REV. CONRAD HUMBERT, J.C.D., Canonical Provisions for Catholic Schools, VII-211 pp., 1939.
118. PARSONS, REV. ANSCAR JOHN, O.M.Cap., J.C.D., Canonical Elections, XII-236 pp., 1939.
119. REILLY, REV. EDWARD MICHAEL, A.B., J.C.D., The General Norms of Dispensation, XII-156 pp., 1939.
120. RYAN, REV. GERALD ALOYSIUS, A.B., J.C.D., Principles of Episcopal Jurisdiction, XII-172 pp., 139.
121. BURTON, REV. FRANCIS JAMES, C.S.C., A.B., J.C.D., Commentary on Canon 1125, X-222 pp., 1940.
122. MIASKIEWICS, REV. FRANCIS SIGISMUND, J.C.D., Supplied Jurisdiction According to Canon 209, XII- 340 pp. 1940.
123. RICE, REV. PATRICK WILLIAM, A.B., J.C.D., Proof of Death in Prenuptial Investigation, VIII-156 pp., 1940.
124. ANGLIN, REV. THOMAS FRANCIS, M.S., J.C.D., The Eucharistic Fast, VIII-183 pp., 1941.
125. COLEMAN, REV. JOHN JEROME, J.C.D., The Minister of Confirmation, VI-153 pp., 1941.
126. DOWNS, REV. JOHN EMMANUEL, A.B., J.C.D., The Concept of Clerical Immunity, XI-163 pp., 1941.
127. ESSWEIN, REV. ANTHONY ALBERT, J.C.D., Extrajudicial Penal Powers of Ecclesiastical Superiors, X-144 pp., 1941.
128. FARRELL, REV. BENJAMIN FRANCIS, M.A., S.T.L., J.C.D., The Rights and Duties of the Local Ordinary Regarding Congregations of Women Religious of Pontifical Approval, V-195 pp., 1941.
129. FEENEY, REV. THOMAS JOHN, A.B., S.T.L., J.C.D., Restitutio in Integrum, VI-169 pp., 1941.
130. FINDLAY, REV. STEPHEN WILLIAM, O.S.B., A.B., J.C.D., Canonical Norms Governing the Deposition and Degradation of Clerics, XVII-279 pp., 1941.
131. GOODWINE, REV. JOHN, A. B., S.T.L., J.C.D., The Right of the Church to Acquire Property, VIII-119 pp., 1941.
132. HESTON, REV. EDWARD LOUIS, C.S.C., Ph.D., S.T.D., J.C.D., The Alienation of Church Property in the United States, XII-222 pp., 1941.
133. HOGAN, REV. JAMES JOHN, A.B., S.T.L., J.C.D., Judicial Advocates and Procurators, XIII-200 pp., 1941.
134. KEALY, REV. THOMAS M., A.B., Litt. B., J.C.D., Dowry of Women Religious, IX-152 pp., 1941.
135. KEENE, REV. MICHAEL JAMES, O.S.B., J.C.D., Religious Ordinaries and Canon 198, V-164 pp., 1941 (printed 1942).
136. KERIN, REV. CHARLES A., S.S., M.A., S.T.B., J.C.D., The Privation of Christian Burial, XVI-279 pp., 1941.

137. LOUIS, REV. WILLIAM FRANCIS, M.A., J.C.D., Diocesan Archives, X-101 pp., 1941.
138. McDEVITT, REV. GILBERT JOSEPH, A.B., J.C.D., Legitimacy and Legitimation, X-247 pp., 1941.
139. McDONOUGH, REV. THOMAS JOSEPH, A.B., J.C.D., Apostolic Administrators, X-217 pp., 1941.
140. MEIER, REV. CARL ANTHONY, A.B., J.C., Penal Administrative Procedure Against Negligent Pastors, XI-240 pp., 1941.
141. SCHMIDT, REV. JOHN ROGG, A.B., J.C.D., The Principles of Authentic Interpretation in Canon 17 of the Code of Canon Law, XII-331 pp., 1941.
142. SLAFKOSKY, REV. ANDREW LEONARD, A.B., J.C.D., The Canonical Episcopal Visitation of the Diocese, X-197 pp., 1941.
143. SWOBODA, REV. INNOCENT ROBERT, O.F.M., J.C.D., Ignorance in Relation to the Imputability of Delicts, IX-271 pp., 1941.
144. DUBE, REV. ARTHUR JOSEPH, A. B., J.C.D., The General Principles for the Reckoning of Time in Canon Law, VIII-299 pp., 1941.
145. McBRIDE, REV. JAMES T., A.B., J.C.D., Incardination and Excardination of Seculars, XX-585 pp., 1941.
146. KROL, REV. JOHN T., J.C.D., The Defendant in Ecclesiastical Trials, XII-207 pp., 142.
147. COMYNS, REV. JOSEPH J., C.SS.R., A.B., J.C.D., Papal and Episcopal Administration of Church Property, XIV-155 pp., 1942.
148. BARRY, REV. GARRETT FRANCIS, O.M.I., J.C.D., Violation of the Cloister, XII-260 pp., 1942.
149. BOLDUC, REV. GATIEN, C.S.V., A. B., S.T.L., J.C.D.,, Les Etudes dans les Religious Clericales, VIII-155 pp., 1942.
150. BOYLE, REV. DAVID JOHN, M.A., J.C.D., The Juridic Effects of Moral Certitude on Pre-Nuptial Guarantees, XII-188 pp., 1942.
151. CANAVAN, REV. WALTER JOSEPH, M.A., Litt.D., J.C.D., The Profession of Faith, XII-143 pp., 1942.
152. DESROCHERS, REV. BRUNO, A.B., Ph.L., S.T.B., J.C.D., Le Premier Concile Plénier de Québec et le Code de Droit Canonique, XIV-186 pp., 1942.
153. DILLON, REV. ROBERT EDWARD, A.B., J.C.D., Common Law Marriage, X-148 pp., 1942.
154. DODWELL, REV. EDWARD JOHN, Ph.D., S.T.B., J.C.D., The Time and Place for the Celebration of Marriage, X-156 pp., 1942.

155. DONNELLAN, REV. THOMAS ANDREW, A.B., J.C.D., The Obligation of the Missa pro Populo, VII-131 pp., 1942.
156. ELTZ, REV. LOUIS ANTHONY, A.B., J.C.D., Cooperation in Crime, XII-208 pp., 1942.
157. GASS, REV. SYLVESTER FRANCIS, M.A., J.C.D., Ecclesiastical Pensions, XI-206 pp., 1942.
158. GUINIVEN, REV. JOHN JOSEPH, C.SS.R., J.C.D., The Precept of Hearing Mass, XIV-188 pp., 1942.
159. GULCZYNSKI, REV. JOHN THEOPHILUS, J.C.D., The Desecration and Violation of Churches, X-126 pp., 1942.
160. HAMILL, REV. JOHN LEO, M.A., J.C.D., The Obligation of the Traveler According to Canon 14, VIII-204 pp., 1942.
161. HAYDT, REV. JOHN JOSEPH, A.B., J.C.D., Reserved Beneficies, XI-148 pp., 1942.
162. HUSER, REV. ROGER JOHN, O.F.M., A.B., J.C.D., The Crime of Abortion in Canon Law, XII-187 pp., 1942.
163. KEARNEY, REV. FRANCIS PATRICK, A.B., S.T.L., J.C.D., The Principles of Canon 1127, X-162 pp., 1942.
164. LINAHEN, REV. LEO JAMES, S.T.L., J.C.D., De Absolutione Complicis in Peccato Turpi, V-114 pp., 1942.
165. McCLOSKEY, REV. JOSEPH ALOYSIUS, A.B., J.C.D., The Subject of Ecclesiastical Law According to Canon 12, XVII-246 pp., 1942 (printed 1943).
166. O'NEILL, REV. FRANCIS JOSEPH, C.SS.R., J.C.D., The Dismissal of Religious in Temporary Vows, XIII-220 pp., 1942.
166. PRINE, REV. JOHN EDWARD, A.B., S.T.B., J.C.D., The Diocesan Chancellor, X-136 pp., 1942.
168. RIESNER, REV. ALBERT JOSEPH, C.SS.R., J.C.D., Apostates and Fugitives from Religious Institutes, IX-168 pp., 1942.
169. STENGER, REV. JOSEPH BERNARD, J.C.D., The Mortgaging of Church Property, 186 pp., 1942.
170. WALDRON, REV., JOSEPH FRANCIS, A.B., J.C.D., The Minister of Baptism, XII-197 pp., 1942.
171. WILLET, REV. ROBERT ALBERT, J.C.D., The Probative Value of Documents in Ecclesiastical Trials, X-124 pp., 1942.
172. WOEBER, REV. EDWARD MARTIN, M.A., J.C.D., The Interpellations, XII-161 pp., 1942.
173. BENKO. REV. MATTHEW ALOYSIUS, O.S.B., M.A., J.C.D., The Abbot Nullius, XVI-148 pp., 1943.
174. CHRIST, REV. JOSEPH JAMES, M.A., S.T.L., J.C.D., Dispensation from Vindicative Penalties, XIV-285 pp., 1943.
175. CLANCY, REV. PATRICK M. J., O.P., A.B., S.T.Lr., J.C.D., The Local Religious Superior, X-229 pp., 1943.
176. CLARKE, REV. THOMAS JAMES, J.C.D., Parish Societies, XII-147 pp., 1943.

177. CONNOLLY, REV. JOHN PATRICK, S.T.L. J.C.D., Synodal Examiners and Parish Priest Consultors, X-223 pp., 1943.
178. DRUMM, REV. WILLIAM MARTIN, A.B., J.C.D., Hospital Chaplains, XII-175 pp., 1943.
179. FLANAGAN, REV. BERNARD JOSEPH, A.B., S.T.L., J.C.D., The Canonical Erection of Religious Houses, X-147 pp., 1943.
180. KELLEHER, REV. STEPHEN JOSEPH, A.B., S.T.B., J.C.D., Discussions with Non-Catholics: Canonical Legislation, X-93 pp., 1943.
181. LEWIS, REV. GORDIAN, C.P., J.C.D., Chapters in Religion Institutes, XII-169 pp., 1943.
182. MARX, REV. ADOLPH, J.C.D., The Declaration of Nullity of Marriages Contracted Outside the Church, X-151 pp., 1943.
183. MATULENAS, REV. RAYMOND ANTHONY, O.S.B., A.B., J.C.D., Communication, a Source of Privileges, VII-225 pp., 1943.
184. O'LEARY, REV. CHARLES GERARD, C.SS.R., J.C.D., Religious Dismissed After Perpetual Profession, X-213 pp., 1943.
185. POWER, REV. CORNELIUS MICHAEL, J.C.D., The Blessing of Cemeteries, XII-231 pp., 1943.
186. SHUHLER, REV. RALPH VINCENT, I.S.A., J.C.D., Privileges of Religious to Absolve and Dispense, XII-195 pp., 1943.
187. ZIOLKOWSKI, REV. THADDEUS STANISLAUS, A.B., J.C.D., The Consecration and Blessing of Churches, XII-151 pp., 1943
188. HENEGHAN, REV. JOHN JOSEPH, S.T.D., J.C.D., The Marriages of Unworthy Catholics: Canons 1065 and 1066, XVI-213 pp., 1944.
189. CARROLL, REV. COLEMAN FRANCIS, M.A., S.T.L., J.C.L., Charitable Institutions.
190. CIESLUK, REV., JOSEPH EDWARD, Ph.B., S.T.L., J.C.D., National Parishes in the United States, VI-178 pp., 1944.
191. COBURN, REV. VINCENT PAUL, A.B., J.C.D., Marriages of Conscience, XII-172 pp., 1944.
192. CONNORS, REV. CHARLES PAUL, C.S.Sp., A.B., J.C.D., Extra-Judicial Procurators in the Code of Canon Law, X-94 pp., 1944.
193. COYLE, REV. PAUL RAYMOND, A.B., J.C.D., Judicial Exceptions, X-142 pp., 1944.
194. FAIR, REV. BARTHOLOMEW FRANCIS, A.B., S.T.L., J.C.D., The Impediment of Abduction, XII-122 pp., 1944.
195. GALLAGHER, REV. THOMAS RAPHAEL, O.P., A.B., S.T.Lr., J.C.D., The Examination of the Qualities of the Ordinand, X-166 pp., 1944.
196. GANNON, REV. JOHN MARK, S.T.L., J.C.D., The Interstices Required for the Promotion to Orders, XII-100 pp., 1944.

197. GOLDSMITH, REV. J. WILLIAM, B.C.S., S.T.L., J.C.D., The Competence of Church and State Over Marriages—Disputed Points, X-128 pp., 1944.
198. GOODWINE, REV. JOSEPH GERARD, A.B., S.T.B., J.C.D. The Reception of Converts, XIV-326 pp., 1944.
199. KOWOLSKI, REV. ROMUALD EUGENE, O.F.M., A.B., J.C.D., Sustenance of Religious Houses of Regulars, X-174 pp., 1944.
200. McCOY, REV. ALAN EDWARD, O.F.M., J.C.D., Force and Fear in Relation to Delictual Imputability and Penal Responsibility, XII-160 pp., 1944.
201. McDEVITT REV. VINCENT JOHN, Ph.D., S.T.L., J.C.L., Perjury.
202. MARTIN, REV. THOMAS OWEN, Ph.D., S.T.D., J.C.D., Adverse Possession, Prescription and Limitation of Actions: The Canonical "Praescriptio," XX-208 pp., 1944.
203. MIKLOSOVIC, REV. PAUL JOHN, A.B., J.C.L., Attempted Marriages and Their Consequent Juridic Effects.
204. MUNDY, REV. THOMAS MAURICE, A.B., S.T.L., J.C.D., The Union of Parishes, X-164 pp., 1944.
205. O'DEA, REV. JOHN COYLE, A. B., J. C. D., The Matrimonial Impediment of Nonage, VIII-126 pp., 1944.
206. OLALIA, REV. ALEXANDER AYSON, S.T.L., J.C.D., A Comparative Study of the Christian Constitution of States and the Constitution of the Philippine Commonwealth, XII-136 pp., 1944.
207. POISSON, REV. PIERRE-MARIE, C.S.C., A.B., Ph.L., Th.L., J.C.L., Droits Patrimoniaux des Maisons et des Eglises Religieuses.
208. STADALNIKAS, REV. CASIMIR JOSEPH, M.I.C., J.C.D., Reservation of Censures, X-141 pp. 1944.
209. SULLIVAN, REV., EUGENE HENRY, S.T.L., J.C.D., Proof of the Reception of the Sacraments, X-165 pp., 1944.
210. VAUGHAN, REV. WILLIAM EDWARD, J.C.D., Constitutions for Diocesan Courts, X-200 pp., 1944.
211. PARO, REV. GINO, S.T.D., J.C.D., The Right of Papal Legation, X-221 pp., 1944 (printed 1947.).
212. BALZER, REV. RALPH FRANCIS, C.P., J.C.D., The Computation of Time in a Canonical Novitiate, X-227 pp., 1945.
213. DOUGHERTY, REV. JOHN WHELAN, A.B., S.T.L., J.C.D., De Inquisitione Speciali, XII-195 pp., 1945.
214. DZIOB, REV. MICHAEL WALTER, J.C.D., The Sacred Congregation for the Oriental Church, XII-181 pp., 1945.
215. EIDENSCHINK, REV. JOHN ALBERT, O.S.B., B.A., J.C.D.,

The Election of Bishops in the Letters of Pope Gregory the Great, VIII-200 pp., 1945.

216. GILL, REV. NICHOLAS, C.P., J.C.D., The Spiritual Prefect in Clerical Religious Houses of Study, X-140 pp., 1945.

217. HYNES, REV. HARRY GERARD, S.T.L., J.C.D., The Privileges of Cardinals, XII-183 pp., 1945.

218. McDEVITT REV. GERALD VINCENT, S.T.L., J.C.D., The Renunciation of an Ecclesiastical Office, XIV-179 pp., 1945.

219. MANNING, REV. JOSEPH LEROY, J.C.D., The Free Conferral of Offices, VII-116 pp., 1945.

220. MEYER, REV. LOUIS G., O.S.B., A.B., S.T.B., J.C.D., Almsgathering by Religious, XII-163 pp., 1945.

221. O'DONNELL, REV. CLETUS FRANCIS, M.A., J.C.D., The Marriage of Minors, XII-268 pp., 1945.

222. PRUNSKIS, REV. JOSEPH, J.C.D., Comparative Law, Ecclesiastical and Civil, in Lithuanian Concordat, X-161 pp., 1945.

223. SWEENEY, REV. FRANCIS PATRICK, C.SS.R.,, The Reduction of Clerics to the Lay State, X-199 pp., 1945.

224. VOGELPOHL, REV. HENRY JOHN, J.C.D., The Simple Impediments to Holy Orders, XVI-190 pp., 1945.

225. BROCKHAUS, REV. THOMAS AQUINAS, O.S.B., J.C.D., Religious who are known as CONVERSI, X-127 pp., 1945.

226. GRIESE, REV. ORVILLE NICHOLAS, S.T.D., J.C.D., The Marriage Contract and the Procreation of Offspring, XVI-224 pp., 1946.

227. BOUDREAUX, REV. WARREN LOUIS, J.C.D., The *"ab acatholics nati"* of Canon 1099, § 2, XII-110 pp., 1946.

228. BOWE, REV. THOMAS JOSEPH, A.B., J.C.D., Religious Superioresses VIII-206 pp., 1946.

229. DIEDERICHS, REV. MICHAEL FERDINAND, S.C.J., J.C.D., The Jurisdiction of the Latin Ordinaries over their Oriental Subjects, XIV-153 pp., 1946.

230. DINGMAN, REV. MAURICE JOHN, A.B., S.T.L., J.C.L., The Plaintiff in Contentious Trials.

231. FAISON. REV. BASIL. C.M.F.. M.Mus.. J.C.D.. The Retroactivity of Law -221 pp., 1946.

232. GALVIN, REV. WILLIAM ANTHONY, M.A., J.C.D., The Administrative Transfer of Pastors, II-288 pp., 1946.

233. GORACY, REV. JOSEPH C., J.C.L., The Diriment Matrimonial Impediment of Major Orders.

234. HALE, REV. JOSEPH FRANCIS, M.A., S.T.L., J.C.D., The Pastor of Burial, X-247 pp., 1946 (printed 1949).

235. HENRY, REV. JOSEPH ARTHUR, A.B., J.C.D., The Mass and Holy Communion: Interritual Law, XII-138 pp., 1946.

236. LINENBERGER, REV. HERBERT, C.PP.S., J.C.D., The False Denunciation of an Innocent Confessor, VIII-205 pp., 1946 (printed 1949).

237. LOWRY, REV. JAMES MARTIN, A.B., J.C.D., Dispensation from Private Vows, XII-266 pp., 1946.

238. LYNCH, REV. GEORGE EDWARD, A.B., S.T.L., J.C.D., Coadjutors and Auxiliaries of Bishops, X-107 pp., 1946 (printed 1947).

239. LYNCH, REV. TIMOTHY, M.S.SS.T., J.C.D., Contracts between Bishops and Religious Congregations, XIII-232 pp., 1946.

240. McCLUNN, REV. JUSTIN DAVID, A.B., S.T.L., J.C.D., Administrative Recourse, VII-142 pp., 1946.

241. LOHMULLER, REV. MARTIN NICHOLAS, A.B., J.C.D., The Promulgation of Law, XII-140 pp., 1947.

242. McGRATH, REV. JAMES, A.B., J.C.D., The Privilege of the Canon, XII-156 pp., 1946.

243. MARBACH, REV. JOSEPH FRANCIS, A.B., J.C.D., Marriage Legislation for the Catholics of the Oriental Rites in the United States and Canada, XIV-314 pp., 1946.

244. SHIMKUS, REV. BERNARD ALOYSIUS, A.B., J.C.L., The Determination and Transfer of Rite.

245. SMITH, REV. VINCENT MICHAEL, A.B., S.T.L., J.C.D., Ignorance Affecting Matrimonial Consent, X-118 pp., 1946 printed 1950).

246. WACHTRLE, REV. PAUL ANTHONY, A. B., J.C.L., The Baptism of the Children of Non-Catholics.

247. CROTTY, REV. MATTHEW MICHAEL, J.C.D., The Recipient of First Holy Communion, X-142 pp., 1947.

248. EAGLETON, REV. GEORGE, J.C.D., The Quinquennial Faculties, Formula IV, XIV-199 pp., 1947 (printed 1948).

249. GIBBONS, REV. MARION LEO, C.M., J.C.L., Domicile of the Wife Unlawfully Separated from Her Husband, XIV-171 pp., 1947.

250. KELLY, REV. BERNARD M., S.T.L., J.C.D., The Functions Reserved to Pastors, XII-141 pp., 1947.

251. KILCULLEN, REV. THOMAS J., LL.M., J.C.D., The Collegiate Moral Person as Party Litigant, X-150 pp., 1947.

252. LAFONTAINE, REV. GERMAINE JOSEPH, W.F., J.C.D., Relations Canoniques entre le Missionaire et Ses Superieurs, X-117 pp., 1947.

253. LANE, REV. LORAS THOMAS, A.B., S.T.L., J.C.D., Matrimonial Procedure in the Ordinary Court of Second Instance, XVI-184 pp., 1947.
254. LOVER, REV. JAMES FRANCIS, C.SS.R., J.C.D., The Master of Novices, X-168 pp., 1947.
255. McNICHOLAS, REV. TIMOTHY JOSEPH, J.C.D., The *Septimae Manus* Witness, XII-133 pp. 1947 (printed 1949).
256. MAROSITZ, REV. JOSEPH JOHN, M.S.C., J.C.D., Obligations and Privileges of Religious Promoted to the Episcopal or Cardinalitial Dignities, XII-180 pp., 1947.
257. MURPHY, REV. FRANCIS JOSEPH, J.C.D., Legislative Powers of the Provincial Council, XII-158 pp., 1947.
258. O'BRIEN, REV. ROMAEUS WILLIAM, O.CARM., J.C.D., The Provincial Superior in Religious Orders of Men, X-294 pp., 1947.
259. PFALLER, REV. BENEDICT ANTHONY, O.S.B., J.C.D., *The ipso acto* Effected Dismissal of Religious, XII-225 pp., 1947.
260. POPEK, REV. ALPHONSE SYLVESTER, J.C.D., The Rights and Obligations of Metropolitans, XX-460 pp., 1947.
261. RISTUCCIA, REV. BERNARD JOSEPH, C.M., J.C.D., Quasi-Religious, XVI-318 pp., 1947 (printed 1949).
262. SONNTAG, REV. NATHANIEL LOUIS, O.F.M.,Cap., J.C.D., Censorship of Special Classes of Books, XII-147 pp., 1947.
263. STADLER, REV. JOSEPH NICHOLAS, J.C.D., Frequent Holy Communion, X-158 pp., 1947.
264. SZAL, REV. IGNATIUS JOSEPH, J.C.D., The Communication of Catholics with Schismatics, XII-217 pp., 1947.
265. WAGNER, REV. URBAN S., O.F.M., Conv. J.C.D., Parochial Substitute Vicars and Supplying Priests, IX-126 pp., 1947.
266. QUINN, REV. JOSEPH, M.A., J.C.D., Documents Required for the Reception of Orders, XIV-207 pp. 1948.
267. BENNINGTON, REV. JAMES CLEMENT, A.B., J.C.L., The Recipient of Confirmation.
268. BLAHER, REV. DAMIAN JOSEPH, O.F.M., A.B., J.C.D., The Ordinary Processes in Causes of Beatification and Canonization, XVI-290 pp., 1948 (printed 1949).
269. CLUNE, REV. ROBERT BELL, B.A., J.C.D., The Judicial Interrogation or the Parties, XII-142 pp., 1948.
270. COURTEMANCHE, REV. BASIL F., B.A., J.C.D., The Total Simulation fo Matrimonial Consent, XX-120 pp., 1948.
271. DLOUHY, REV. MAUR JOHN, O.S.B., A.B., J.C.L., The Ordination of Exempt Religious.
272. DONOVAN, REV. JOHN THOMAS, Ph.B., S.T.L., J.C.D., The Clerical Obligation of Canons 138 and 140, XII-209 pp., 1948.

273. FREKING, REV. FREDERICK W., A.B., S.T.B., J.C.D., The Canonical Installation of Pastors, XII-210 pp., 1948.
274. FULTON, REV. THOMAS B., J.C.D., Prenuptial Investigation, XII-190 pp., 1948.
275. GODLEY, REV. JAMES P., J.C.D., Time and Place for the Celebration of Mass, X-206 pp., 1948 (printed 1949).
276. KANE, REV. THOMAS A., A.B., B.S., J.C.D., The Jurisdiction of the Patriarchs of the Major Sees in Antiquity and in the Middle Ages, XII-111 pp., 1948 (printed 1949).
277. KENNEDY, REV. ANDREW A., J.C.L., The Annual Pastoral Report to the Local Ordinary.
278. KONRAD, REV. JOSEPH GEORGE, J.C.D., Transfer of Religious to Another Community, VIII-284 pp., 1948 (printed 1949).
279. KRESS, REV. ALPHONSE, J.C.L., Contumacy in Ecclesiastical Trials.
280. McCARTNEY, REV. MARCELLUS ANTHONY, O.F.M., M.A., J.C.D., Faculties of Regular Confessors, XII-164 pp., 1948 (printed 1949).
281. McCASLIN, REV. EDWARD PATRICK, M.A., S.T.L., J.C.L., The Division of Parishes.
282. McELROY, REV. FRANCIS J., A.B., J.C.D., The Privileges of Bishops, XII-142 pp., 1948 (printed 1951).
283. QUINN, REV. STEPHEN, M.S.SS.T., J.C.D., Relation Between the Local Ordinary and Religious of Diocesan Approval. XII-153 pp., 1948 (printed 1949).
284. SCHNEIDER, REV. EDELHARD LOUIS, S.D.C., B.A., J.C.L., The Status of Secularized Ex-Religious Clerics, X-155 pp., 1948.
285. THOMPSON, CHESTER J., A.B., J.C.D., The Simple Removal from Office, XII-141 pp., 1948 (printed 1951).
286. O'BRIEN, REV. KENNETH R., A.B., J.C.D., The Nature of Support of Diocesan Priests in the United States, XVI-162 pp., 1949.
287. METZ, REV. JOHN E., S.T.L., J.C.D., The Recording Judge in the Ecclesiastical Collegiate Tribunal, X-130 pp., 1949.
288. REINHARDT, REV. MARION J., S.T.L., J.C.D., The Rogatory Commission, XIII-182 pp., 1949.
289. ORTEGA, UHIUK, REV. JUAN, S.J., J.C.L., De Delicto Socitationis.
290. CASEY, REV. JAMES V., J.C.D., A Study of Canon 2222 § 1, XII-127 pp., 1949.
291. ALLGEIR, REV. JOSEPH L., J.C.D., The Canonical Obligation of Preaching in Parish Churches, X-115 pp., 1949 (printed 1950).

292. CAHILL, REV. DANIEL R., J.C.D., The Custody of the Holy Eucharist, XVI-178 pp., 1949 (printed 1950).

293. CARR, REV. AIDEN, O.F.M., Conv., S.T.D., J.C.D., Vocation to the Prisethood: Its Canonical Concept, VIII-124 pp., 1949 (printed 1950).

294. KNOPKE, REV. ROCH F., O.F.M., J.C.D., Reverential Fear in Matrimonial Cases in Asiatic Countries: Rota Cases, XII-112 pp., 1949.

295. LAVELLE, REV. HOWARD D., J.C.D., The Obligation of Holding Sacred Missions in Parishes, XVI-142 pp., 1949.

296. MICKELLS, REV. ANTHONY B., J.C.D., The Constitutive Elements of Parishes, X-145 pp., 1949 (printed 1950).

297. NOONE, REV. JOHN J., J.C.D., Nullity in Judicial Acts, X-147 pp., 1949 (printed 1950).

298. SHEEHAN, REV. DANIEL E., J.C.D., The Minister of Holy Communion, X-189 pp., 1949 (printed 1950).

299. STATKUS, REV. FRANCIS J., J.C.D., The Minister of the Last Sacraments, XII-162 pp., 1949 (printed 1950).

300. COOK, REV. JOHN P., J.C.D., Ecclesiastical Communities and Their Ability to Induce Legal Customs, XII-152 pp., 1949 (printed 1950).

301. FAZZALARO, REV. FRANCIS J., J.C.D., The Place for the Hearing of Confessions, X-150 pp., 1949 (printed 1950).

302. HANNAN, REV. PHILIP M., J.C.D., The Canonical Concept of *congrua sustentatio* for the Secular Clergy, XII-237 pp., 1949 (printed 1950).

303. QUINN, REV. HUGH G., J.C.D., The Particular Penal Precept XII-108 pp., 1953.

304. GALLAGHER, REV. JOHN F., J.C.L., The Matrimonial Impediment of Public Propriety.

305. WELSH, REV. THOMAS J., J.C.D., The Use of the Portable Altar, XII-141 pp., 1949 (printed 1950).

www.ingramcontent.com/pod-product-compliance
Lightning Source LLC
LaVergne TN
LVHW050202080826
844660LV00012B/335
9780813224794